SHORT STIRLING in action

By Ron Mackay

Color By Don Greer
Illustrated By Perry Manley

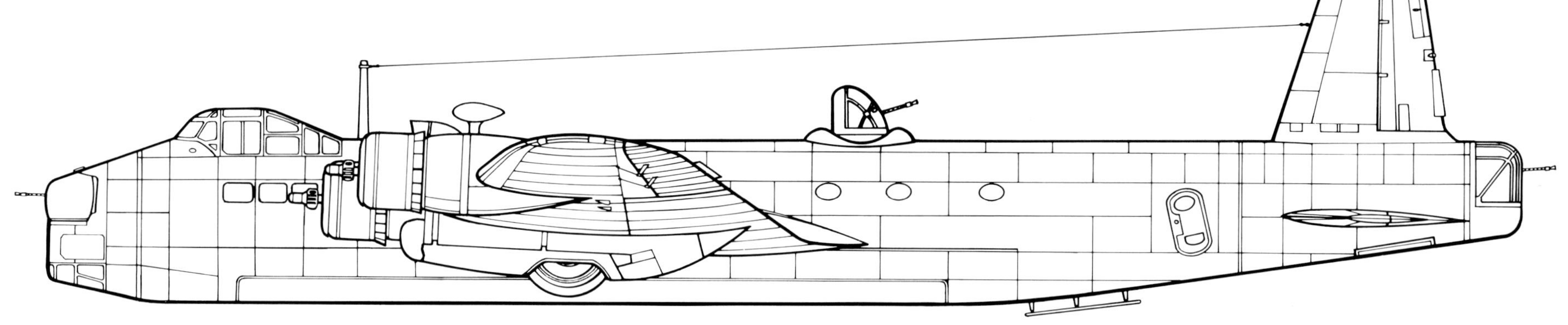

Aircraft Number 96
squadron/signal publications

A pair of Stirling Mk IIIs of No 15 Squadron enroute to a bombing mission over Remscheid, Germany, on the night of 30/31 July 1943. Stirlings operated mainly in the night bombing role over Germany.

COPYRIGHT © 1989 SQUADRON/SIGNAL PUBLICATIONS, INC.
1115 CROWLEY DRIVE CARROLLTON, TEXAS 75011-5010
All rights reserved. No part of this publication may be reproduced, stored in a retrieval system or transmitted in any form by any means electrical, mechanical or otherwise, without written permission of the publisher.

ISBN 0-89747-228-4

If you have any photographs of the aircraft, armor, soldiers or ships of any nation, particularly wartime snapshots, why not share them with us and help make Squadron/Signal's books all the more interesting and complete in the future. Any photograph sent to us will be copied and the original returned. The donor will be fully credited for any photos used. Please send them to:

Squadron/Signal Publications, Inc.
1115 Crowley Drive.
Carrollton, TX 75011-5010.

Photo Credits

Short Brothers
Bruce Robertson
Jerry Scutts
Bernard Baines
Eric K. Garnett
Serge Blandin
John Clarke
Darrell Debolt
Don Clarke
George Jeffreys
John Reid
W.H. Steed
I.W.M.
John D.R. Rawlings
R.A.F. Museum
Dick Ward
Peter Baldock
Fred Kreuger
U.S.A.F. Museum
Stirling Aircraft Association
No 90 Squadron Association
Tom Gillan
A.J.B. Harding
Hans-Heiri Stapfer

Dedication

This book is dedicated to Ted Dax, Peter Baldock, Phil Panichelli, Gino Palumbo, Bert Fitchett, Doug Fry and the late W.K. "Bill" Bailey. They, along with many other Commonwealth aircrews, rightfully put their trust in Short's Stirling bomber.

A Stirling Mk I of No 218 Squadron runs up its outboard engine at either Stradishall or Chedburgh, Suffolk during 1942. The aircraft serial (N3725) identifies it as one of the second production batch built at Rochester. This Stirling was later lost on return from Wilhelmshaven on 15 Sept 42 when engine failure caused it to spin in while in the landing pattern.

D HA

INTRODUCTION

Until 1936, the Royal Air Force had operated either single or twin engine bombers; however, the activities of the Americans and Russians in building four engine bomber prototypes led the Air Staff to begin discussions aimed at producing a similar aircraft for the RAF. These discussions led to issuing a specification for the RAF's first four engine bomber under the title Specification B12/36.

Specification B12/36 called for a number of technical requirements that had not been previously attempted in England. The specification required that the aircraft be capable of both normal and catapult assisted takeoffs. It was felt that a catapult assisted takeoff would allow the bomber to carry greater bomb and fuel loads. Under normal takeoff conditions, the aircraft was required to have a range of 1,500 miles with a 2,000 pound bomb load. With catapult assistance, the range went up to 2,000 miles with 14,000 pounds of bombs and 3,000 miles with 8,000 pounds (flying at maximum altitude and at maximum cruise).

The specification called for a maximum weight of 31,200 pounds or 36,000 pounds depending on takeoff configuration, a cruising speed of 230 mph and a service ceiling of 28,000 feet. Takeoff runs of 1,500 feet (normal) and 2,100 feet (catapult assisted) were anticipated. The specified capability to use catapult assist for takeoff was not as strange as it might appear. RAF bomber airfields during the 1930s were small, grass covered strips and it was anticipated that these two factors could cause severe problems for heavy bomber operations. The required takeoff run not only reflected the distance required to lift off, but also included a requirement to clear a fifty foot obstacle within 1,500 feet. This would require the use of powerful engines and a large wing span/area.

The specification stated that the largest bomb to be carried by the new bomber would be a 2,000 pound armor piercing weapon, while normal bomb loads would consist of standard RAF pre-war bombs of either 250 or 500 pounds. It was felt that these weapons would be sufficient to deal with a wide range of targets.

Short was one of eleven companies asked to submit proposals based on Specification B12/36. The Short's proposal emerged as a four engine, mid-wing bomber originally to be powered by four liquid cooled Rolls Royce Goshawk engines. The aircraft would have a crew of six; two pilots, an observer/navigator, wireless operator, and two gunners manning the nose and tail turret. Provision was also made for a remote-control turret in the lower portion of the rear fuselage. Armor would be fitted along with sound proofing and even a toilet; however, no inflatable dinghy was initially included in the design (although it was later installed).

By late 1936, the Air Staff had narrowed the competition down to two companies, Short and Supermarine, and fuselage mock-ups were ordered of both designs. During the development of the designs, the distance estimated for the takeoff and landing was strictly watched. The Air Ministry feared that the new bombers would require exceedingly long takeoff and landing runs requiring new airfields to handle them. Acquiring land for new airfields was politically difficult and might lead to cancellation of both projects.

In order to keep the takeoff and landing run within limits, Short's Chief Designer, Mr. Lipcombe, felt that the wing length should be enlarged from under 100 feet to around 112 feet. This request was rejected, with the Air Ministry stating that existing RAF hangars would not accommodate wing spans of more than 100 feet. Additionally, the small size of RAF airfields would restrict movements of such a large aircraft. It should be noted that the C Type hangar was under consideration during 1936 and its door width of 120 feet was more than enough to handle the Short bomber. Regardless, the decision was to create a severe altitude and range limitation because of a decreased wing aspect ratio.

The S31/M4 was a half scale Stirling prototype used to test the aircraft's aerodynamics. The single stage undercarriage fitted to the S31 was later replaced with a two stage undercarriage that was adapted for the second prototype and all production Stirlings.

During 1937, Short completed the fuselage mock-up. It had a length of eighty-seven feet, of which forty-two feet was bomb bays. RAF transportation requirements reportedly limited the four fuselage sub-sections to no more than twenty-five feet. The aircraft's rigid structure was achieved by shaping the fuselage in a semi-rectangular cross section with lower section spars being fitted level with the internal decking. These, in turn, were supported by two longitudinal girders. The presence of these girders in the bomb bay area would restrict each of the three parallel bomb bays to bombs of no more than two feet in width. At the time this was not a critical factor, given the small weight and diameter of the bombs in use. Later, as the war progressed, the need for heavier weapons would leave the Short bomber hopelessly outclassed by its contemporaries, which could handle the largest bombs available.

Short's work on the Sunderland flying boat provided the basis for much of the structure of the new bomber, and nowhere was that influence more obvious than in wing layout. The wing was almost identical to that used on the Sunderland, with the exception of three bomb bays between the fuselage and inner engine nacelle. Fuel capacity was housed in seven wing tanks with a total capacity of 2,254 gallons (an extra 220 gallons could be in ferry tanks installed in the wing bomb bays). All main tanks were self-sealing with the exception of the wing leading edge tanks which were not self-sealing. The outer wing sections were watertight to provide bouyancy in the event of a water landing. Finally, large flaps, designed by Arthur Gouge, were fitted to the wing trailing edge to reduce takeoff and landing runs.

Performance estimates at this stage suggested a top speed of 327 mph and a cruising speed of 282 mph at a maximum weight of 59,090 pounds (8,000 pounds of bombs). As work progressed and the aircraft's weight continued to rise, these figures were revised downward. The cruising speed estimate fell to 263 mph at a maximum weight of 50,536 pounds (2,000 pounds of bombs).

Unlike the Supermarine project, which was centered around a full scale prototype, Short chose to construct a half-scale flying prototype during 1938, which was intended to reveal any aerodynamic problems. Powered by four 90 hp Pobjoy engines and constructed of plywood, the aircraft was officially designated the S31, but was better known as M4. The S31/M4 first flew on 19 September 1938 with Short's Chief Test Pilot John Lankester Parker at the controls. Within a few weeks, the flight tests at the RAF's Aeroplane and Armament Experimental Establishment (A. and A.E.E.) at Martlesham Health in Suffolk had been completed. While generally satisfied, RAF officials expressed concern over the prototype's takeoff and landing runs, which were felt to be excessive. The proposed solution was to almost double the wing angle of incidence from 3 ½ degrees to 6 ½ degrees. Since both planning and tooling for the first production aircraft was at an advanced stage, Short decided to drastically lengthen the undercarriage legs to achieve the required additional 3 degrees of wing incidence.

The single stage landing gear leg was discarded due to the increased length of the undercarriage rods which proved too long to be retracted into the engine nacelle wheel wells. A two stage undercarriage was built which retracted vertically and then backward into the nacelle. The undercarriage retraction motors were originally located inside the nacelle, but were later relocated inside the fuselage to allow for manual retraction in the event of motor failure. The manual undercarriage system required some 740 turns of the crank handle to lower or raise the undercarriage. To handle the aircraft's weight, the tail wheel was comprised of twin wheels rather than the more common single wheel unit found on most bombers.

The revised undercarriage layout was installed on the S31/M4 prototype and the power plants were also changed from the 90 hp Pobjoy engines to 115 hp Niagara IV engines. Horn balances were also added to the elevators. By early 1939, it was becoming apparent that Short was ahead of Supermarine in the Specification B12/36 competition. By this time the Air Ministry had dropped the requirement for catapult takeoffs and had added a requirement for wing leading edge wire cutters to sever barrage balloon cables. While testing resumed with the S31/M4, construction began on two full size prototypes, now officially known as the Stirling Mk I/P1.

Shortly after construction of the prototypes began, the Air Ministry decided to order the Stirling into production with a contract for 100 Stirling Mk Is. The prototype Stirling (given the factory designation S.29) was rolled out of the company's Rochester factory on 13 May 1939. Because of a delay in the availability the Bristol Hercules I engines, the prototype was fitted with four 1,375 hp Bristol Hercules II engines. The prototype was armed with three power gun turrets, a Frazer Nash nose turret with two .303 Browning machine guns, a Frazer Nash tail turret with four .303 Browning machine guns and a retractable Frazer Nash ventral turret with two .303 Brownings.

Given the RAF serial number L7600, the prototype made its maiden flight on 14 May. After a graceful takeoff and short test flight the prototype suffered an undercarriage failure on landing and was damaged beyond repair. The failure was traced to the light alloy undercarriage back arch braces which were replaced on succeeding aircraft by stronger tubular steel units.

The second prototype (L7605) was fitted with the strengthened undercarriage and made its maiden flight on 3 December 1939. For this flight the gear was left down, but happily for both Short and the RAF, the revised undercarriage held up when put to the acid tests of retraction, lowering, and landing. During the Spring of 1940, the prototype spent four months undergoing service tests at Boscombe Down.

During the same time period as these tests, the first production Stirling Mk I (N3637) was being tested by Lankester Parker. During testing, problems were encountered with slow throttle movement, which led to a three engine landing. The Exactor throttles installed in Short flying boats, and used in the Stirling, were prone to moving to the closed position if hand pressure was removed. To solve this problem, serrated arcs of metal were mounted on the throttle box with spring-loaded detents located on the throttle levers which held the throttle handle in the required position. Later the throttles were modified with a hinged top on the throttle levers, which when pulled or pushed, lifted a spring loaded detent; this in turn engaged an adjustable stop, setting the throttles at cruise power.

N3637 followed the second prototype to Boscome Down. Tests at a maximum weight of 57,400 pounds revealed that the Stirling Mk I required a takeoff run of 3,600 feet to clear a fifty foot obstacle (1,920 feet were required to lift off). Maximum speed was 218 mph while the service ceiling was a disappointing 15,000 feet. Stall speed was 107 mph IAS (indicated air speed) and the initial rate of climb was 900 feet per minute (for the first 5,000 feet). Climb rate fell off rapidly above 5,000 feet, and from 10,000 to 15,000 feet the aircraft climbed at a slow 160 feet per minute.

The Stirling prototype (L7600) reveals the high landing gear that became hallmark of the Stirling. National markings carried by the prototype were confined to Type A wing and fuselage roundels. On 14 May 1939, the aircraft made its maiden flight and suffered an undercarriage failure on landing, ending its career.

These test results showed that the Stirling's performance at 12,000 to 13,000 feet was far below the original requirements. It was felt that part of the poor showing in the aircraft's performance was due to the low power of the Hercules II engines. The up rated (1,425 hp) Hercules III engines intended for production aircraft were expected to noticeably improve overall performance.

With the exception of N3644 (which was re-engined with Hercules III engines and released for RAF service) the remainder of the first ten production aircraft were designated as trainers. An interesting feature of these aircraft was the monocoque engine nacelles whose layout was to cause problems for aircraft maintenance crews, especially during engine changes. As a result of this problem, firewalls were installed just ahead of the wing leading edge on all subsequent aircraft, and the engine mounts were modified to ease maintenance.

The first Stirling (L7600) sets on its belly after the undercarriage failed on its first flight. The number 2 engine has been twisted out of its mounting and workmen have removed the propellers from the other engines. The aircraft never flew again and was scrapped.

Development

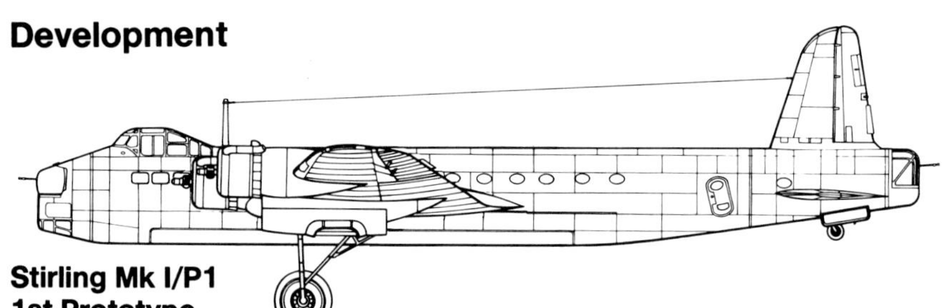

Stirling Mk I/P1
1st Prototype

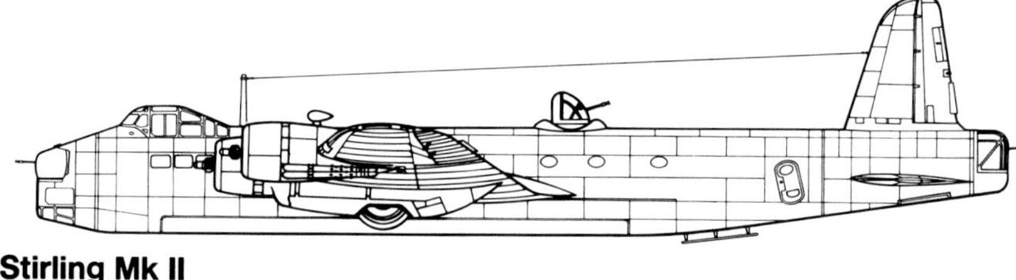

Stirling Mk II

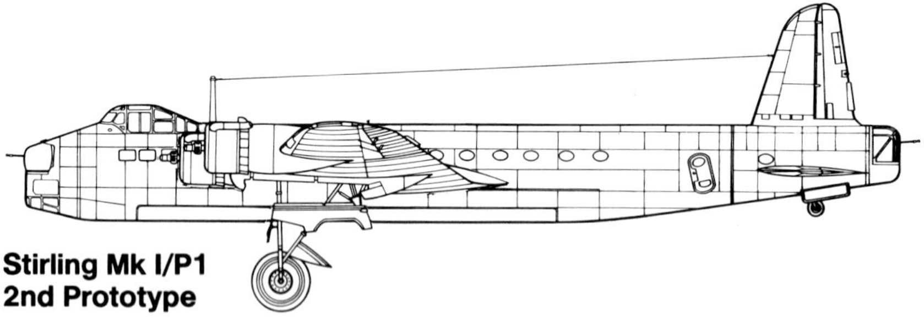

Stirling Mk I/P1
2nd Prototype

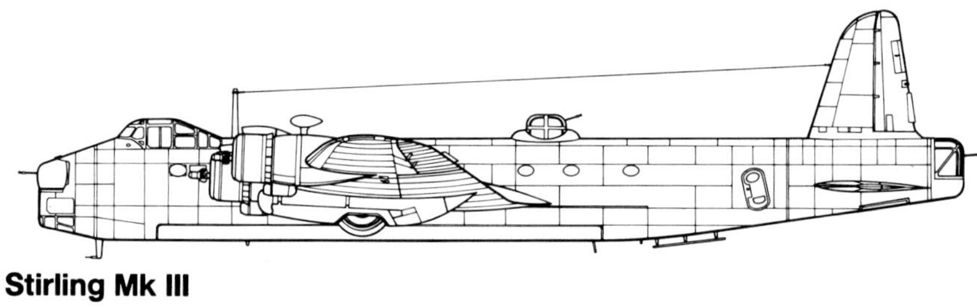

Stirling Mk III

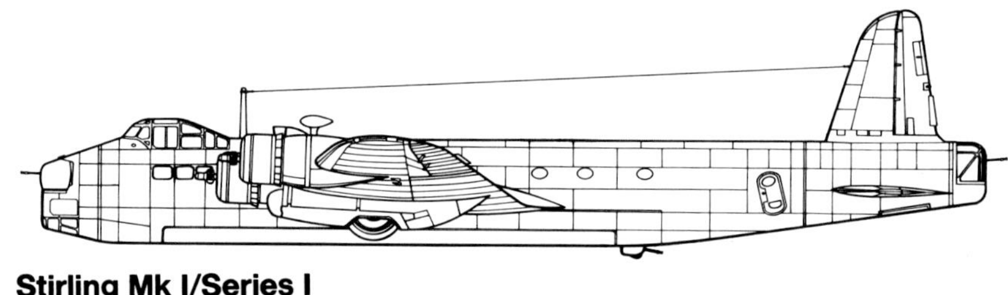

Stirling Mk I/Series I

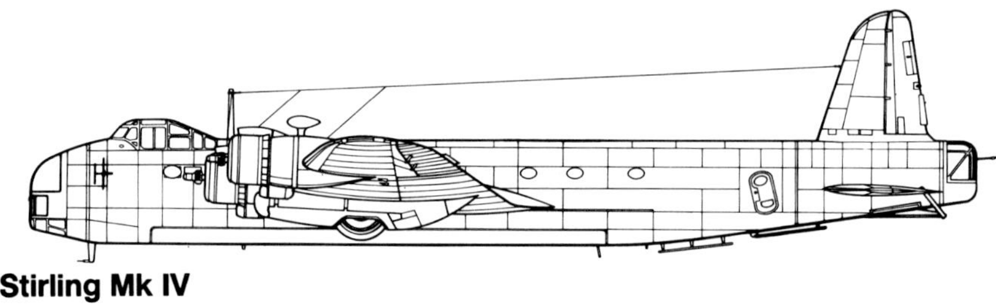

Stirling Mk IV

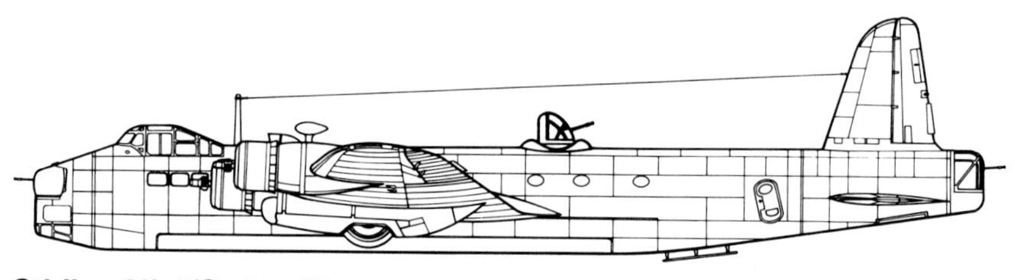

Stirling Mk I/Series III

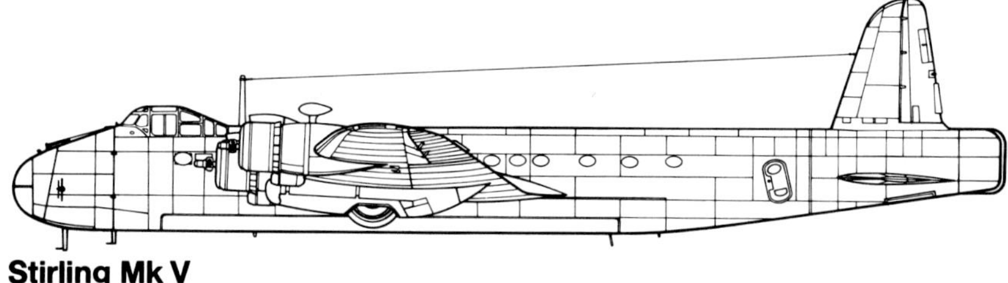

Stirling Mk V

Stirling Mk I

The early production Stirling Mk I differed little from the prototype and featured the strengthened landing gear introduced on the second prototype. Very early production Stirling Mk Is had the engine exhaust stacks of the two port wing engines mounted on the port side of the nacelle, while the starboard wing engines had the stacks on the starboard side of the nacelle. This was soon changed with the stacks of all engines being mounted on the port side of the nacelle. These aircraft were also fitted with propeller spinners which were deleted shortly after production began.

During August of 1940 two events took place that were to have an effect on Stirling production. On 2 August the first production Stirling Mk I was delivered to No 7 Squadron at RAF Leeming, the first squadron to begin conversion to the new bomber. Thirteen days later, on 15 August, Do-17Zs of KG-3 attacked the Short plant at Rochester, Kent. Although the plant itself was not badly damaged, no less than six Stirling Mk Is on the assembly line were destroyed. Luckily this was the only such attack against the Short factory.

The vulnerability of the plant had been recognized earlier, and this, along with a need to increase production, had prompted Short to construct a second plant in Belfast, Northern Ireland. This plant was attacked by He-111s of KG 100 during August, with four Stirlings in the final assembly shop being destroyed. Damage was slight and the first Belfast built Stirling rolled off the assembly line in October.

The bombing of the Rochester plant had highlighted the known vulnerability of the Stirling's primary production source and the decision was made to lessen this vulnerability by dispersing production. Orders were issued for secondary production lines to be set up at Austin Motors in Longbridge and by Rootes at their shadow factory at Stoke-on-Trent. Additionally, a number of component parts were subcontracted to upwards of twenty different firms at various locations throughout Britain, with the co-ordination of this dispersed production effort coming under the Ministry of Aircraft Production. This dispersal plan took some time to implement and in the interim period facilities at Swindon and Huccelcote, along with several sites in the West Country were utilized for dispersed production.

Operational testing of the Stirling Mk Is assigned to No 7 Squadron revealed several problems with the early Stirling Mk I because of their low rated Hercules II engines. The most serious difficulty involved the Exactor throttles, although of almost equal concern was the tendency of the undercarriage retraction motors to burn out. Oil leaks, plug faults, and other small problems began giving the Stirling a reputation of being a maintenance problem.

As a result of these problems, the Stirling was relegated to the non-operational trainer status until its problem areas could be corrected. To cure the throttle problem, it was planned to modify the throttle controls to a more reliable rod-and-chain system which had been designed for installation on the Stirling Mk II. In the event, since introduction of the modification into the Mk I production line would overly disrupt the delivery of Mk I production aircraft to new units, the modification was not made.

During this same period, two Stirling Mk Is (N3635 and N3637) were assigned to test status at Boscombe Down. These tests revealed that at a maximum weight of 64,000 pounds, the takeoff distance was now 4,500 feet and at a maximum weight of 75,400 pounds, the aircraft required some thirty-four minutes to reach its service ceiling. The most economical cruising speed was 165 mph at 10,000 feet, although this low ceiling was considered marginal to penetrate any distance into enemy territory. During this time frame, however, 10,000 feet was the operational altitude of most British bombers (twin engine Wellingtons and Blenheims) and the Stirling's low ceiling was not considered serious.

Defensive armament for the Stirling Mk I differed from the prototype and evolved in three stages, known as Stirling Mk I Series I, II, and III. The Stirling Mk I Series I aircraft carried Frazer Nash nose (FN5A), belly (FN25A) and tail (FN4A) turrets.

The Stirling Mk I Series II deleted the belly turret replacing it with provision for two .303 Browning machine guns on FN55A beam mounts in the fuselage sides (although it is believed that no operational Series II aircraft ever had the beam mounts actually installed). Additionally, the tail turret was replaced with a FN20A turret (equipped with servo feed). The belly turret was removed because it usually slipped downward whenever the aircraft was taxied over rough ground. Additionally, whenever the turret was lowered, the resulting drag caused a definite loss of speed.

The first Series III aircraft was the 81st Stirling off the production line and this aircraft established the standard for Stirling defensive armament. Stirling Mk I Series III aircraft had the defensive armament increased by the addition of a Frazer Nash FN7A dorsal turret armed with twin .303 Browning machine guns. The circular belly turret hatch was retained and fitted with a single hand held flexible .303 gun. Armament now totalled eight .303 machine guns in power driven turrets and a single .303 machine gun in the belly (when carried).

Besides the improved armament, the Series III aircraft were also re-engined with the long awaited 1,500 hp Hercules XI engines which were equipped with two-speed superchargers. The engine change also brought a change in the engine nacelle. The Hercules II engines on the Stirling Mk I Series I were mounted in monocoque nacelles which made engine servicing and engine changes difficult. With the introduction of the new engines, the nacelle was also modified with new internal engine mounts. Two different engine mounts were designed, one by Short and the other by Bristol. Aircraft with the Short designed mounts were classified as part of Series II, while those with the Bristol mounts were included in Series III. Series III aircraft also had the engine exhausts modified with the short exhaust stacks being replaced with flame dampening "barbed" exhaust stacks.

The fourth production Stirling Mk I taxies along the taxiway at Rochester, Short's main production facility. The bomber carries an extended fin flash on the vertical stabilizer, which was a common marking on early Stirling Mk Is. The Black areas on the fin and stabilizer leading edges are rubber deicing boots.

Stirling Mk I N3663 was the first Series III aircraft and tests with this aircraft revealed that the Series III aircraft had a maximum speed of 255 mph at 10,000 feet and 230 mph at 16,000 feet (with supercharging) while at a maximum weight of 70,000 pounds.

The crew complement of the Mk I Series III was seven; two pilots, navigator/bomb-aimer, wireless operator, two gunners and flight engineer. Later in the war the navigator/bomb-aimer duties were split, at which point Stirling crews rose to eight.

The Stirling Mk I had a series of oval windows mounted in the sides of the fuselage. Four windows were located on the port side, and five on the starboard side of the nose area, with another eight on the starboard and nine on the port fuselage sides running from the wing spar to the horizontal stabilizer.

An early production Stirling Mk I Series I of No 7 Squadron shares the ramp with a Supermarine Spitfire at RAF Oakington, home base for No 7 Squadron. Early Stirling Mk Is had the engine exhausts of the port engines mounted high on the port side cowling edge.

An early production Stirling Mk I Series I starts its engines on the ramp at the Short's factory at Rochester, England. Most early Mk Is were underpowered and used in the training role by No 7 Squadron, the first RAF Bomber Command unit to receive the Stirling. The aircraft in the background are Handley Page Herefords.

Engine Nacelles

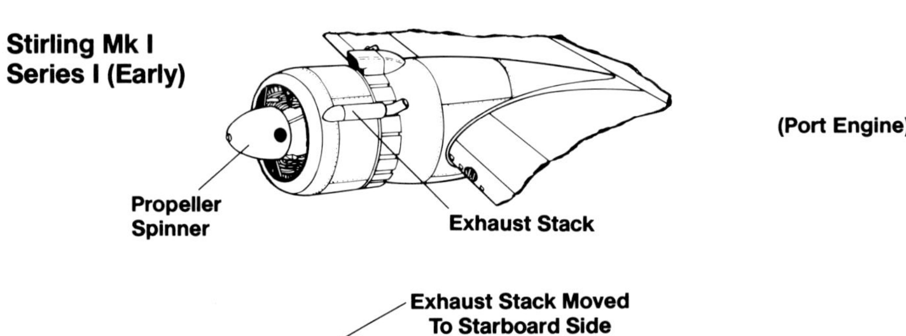

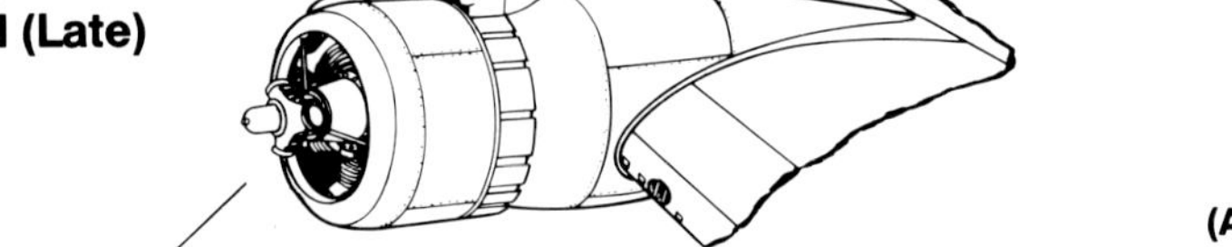

Stirling Mk I
Series I (Late)

(All Engines)

Spinner
Deleted

The lack of a dorsal turret indicates that these Stirling Mk Is on the Rochester production line are part of the Series I production batch. The panels on the wing of the second Stirling reveals the location of the wing fuel tanks. The wing trailing edge curves forward at the wing/fuselage joint, producing a bent look when the flaps are lowered.

The crew of this Stirling Mk I (W7440) have just started the starboard engine. This aircraft was assigned to No 7 Squadron between August of 1941 and May of 1942 before being transferred to a Stirling Conversion Unit. The aircraft in the background is a Wellington of No 101 Squadron.

Ground crews perform maintenance on a Stirling Mk I engine. The oval panels on the wing upper surface are the fuel tank covers which were a carry over from the Sunderland flying boat. The two angled posts near the wing trailing edge are the twin aileron control link cables and rods.

Ground crews refuel a Stirling Mk I from a fuel bowser, which was the standard RAF fuel truck used during the Second World War. The trailer in front of the vehicle was an oil bowser, used to replenish the aircraft's oil tanks. This Stirling Mk I is a later production aircraft with all engine exhausts mounted on the starboard side of the cowl.

The crew of ***MACROBERTS REPLY***, a No 15 Squadron Stirling Mk I, walk away from their aircraft, which had the name carried on the nose in White. The subscriber, Lady MacRoberts, had lost three sons in RAF aircraft, two of them on active operations, and funded this Stirling's cost as in memory of her sons.

After the initial production batch, Stirlings were delivered in standard night bomber camouflage. This Stirling Mk I of No 149 (East India) Squadron at RAF Mildenhall, Suffolk, is a presentation aircraft and carries the name *EAST INDIA 1* on the nose in White. The aircraft was later passed to 1651 HCU at RAF Waterbeach and was scrapped after the undercarriage collapsed on 2 September 1942.

Exhaust Stacks

Stirling Mk I Series I

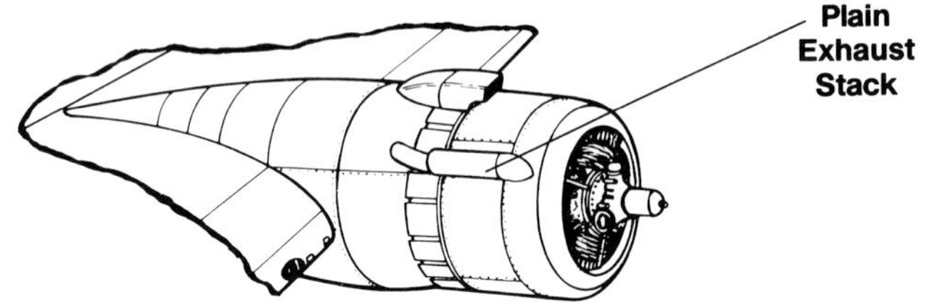

Stirling Mk I Series III

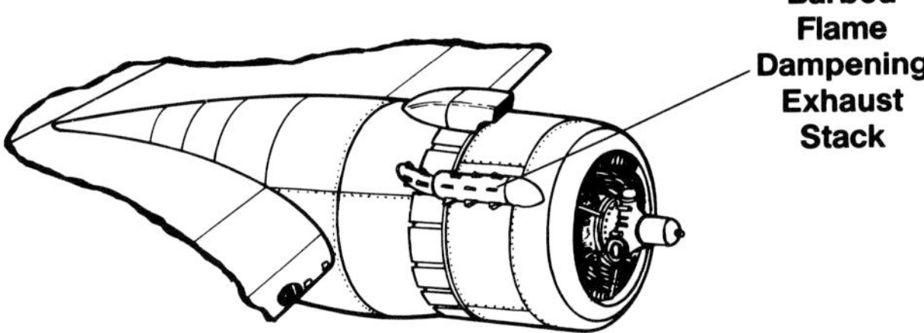

EAST INDIA 1 reveals the starboard side fuselage window layout and frameless FN5A nose turret. The FN5A was armed with two .303 Browning machine guns and remained the standard nose turret carried by all Stirling bombers. The twin pitot tube masts just behind the bomb aimer's windows were also a standard fitting to the Stirling Mk I.

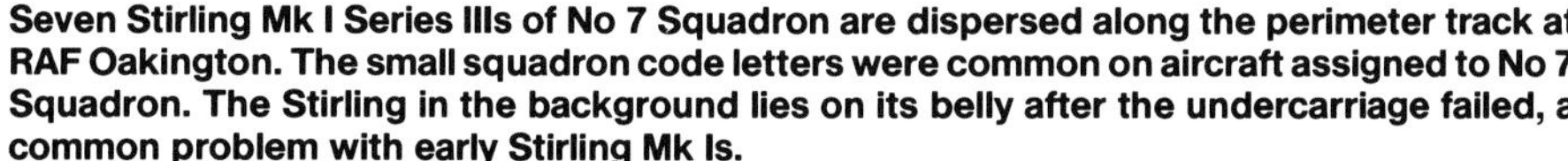
Seven Stirling Mk I Series IIIs of No 7 Squadron are dispersed along the perimeter track at RAF Oakington. The small squadron code letters were common on aircraft assigned to No 7 Squadron. The Stirling in the background lies on its belly after the undercarriage failed, a common problem with early Stirling Mk Is.

King Peter of Yugoslavia (middle) inspects the tail turret of a Stirling Mk I. The Frazer Nash FN20A rear turret was unique to the Stirling. In their fully depressed position, the barrels of the four .303 machine guns barely protrude beyond the cartridge ejection chutes on the bottom of the turret.

The navigator's position in the Stirling was just behind the port pilot's seat, with navigator facing to port, and was equipped with a plotting table and light. This navigator is plotting a course using a Dalton's Computer, the type issued to all RAF navigators.

Outer wing sections were probably the most replaced part on the Stirling because they were often damaged beyond repair when the aircraft suffered an undercarriage failure. This Stirling Mk I Series III of No 7 Squadron had the port undercarriage fail on landing and dug in the port outer wing section.

The two pilot positions of a Stirling Mk I. The seat harness straps on the port (pilot's) seat are visible just at the top of the armored seat. The containers behind the starboard (co-pilot's) seat are probably used to hold signal flares. The crew complement of the Stirling was later changed to a single pilot, reducing the crew to seven.

Turret Locations

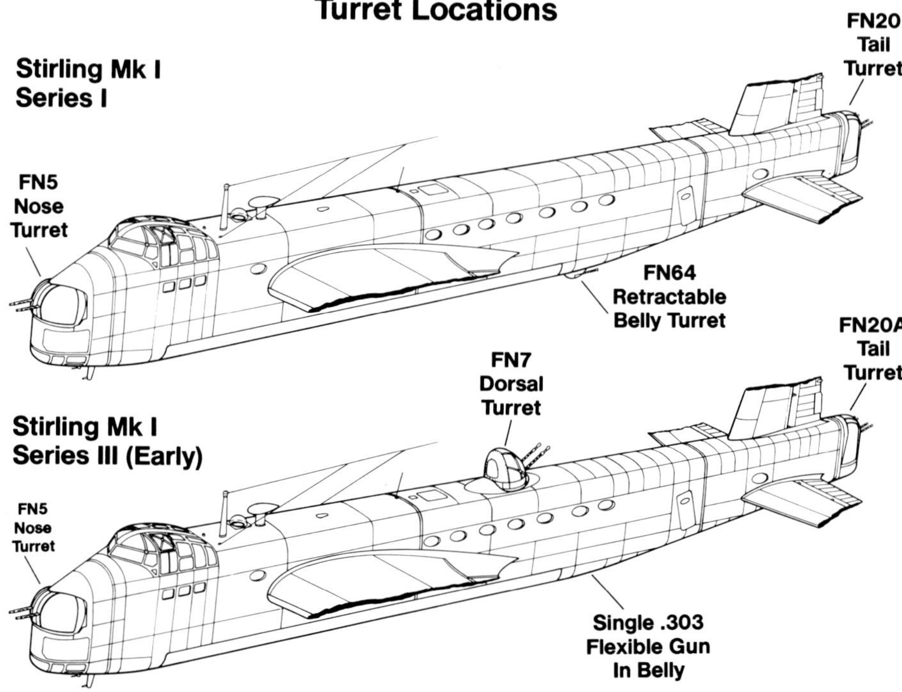

This Stirling Mk I of No 7 Squadron is being loaded with a mixed load of explosive and incendiary bombs. The aircraft is unusual in that it carries standard size code letters on the fuselage side. It was No 7 Squadron's normal practice to use small code letters for the squadron code and a large letter for the individual aircraft code.

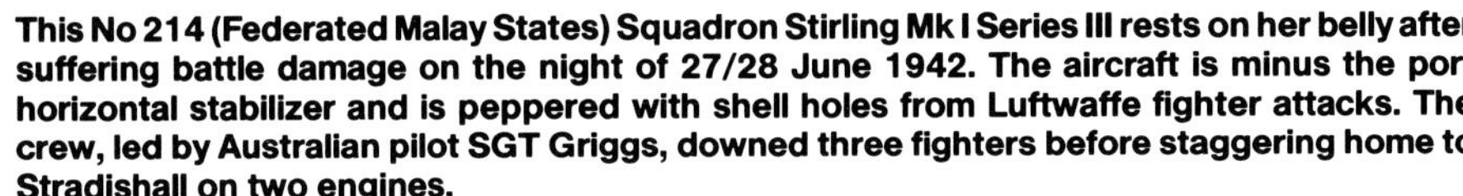

This No 214 (Federated Malay States) Squadron Stirling Mk I Series III rests on her belly after suffering battle damage on the night of 27/28 June 1942. The aircraft is minus the port horizontal stabilizer and is peppered with shell holes from Luftwaffe fighter attacks. The crew, led by Australian pilot SGT Griggs, downed three fighters before staggering home to Stradishall on two engines.

The engines of this Stirling Mk I (N - Nuts) of No 149 Squadron at either Mildenhall or Lakenheath, are run up prior to arming the bomber with its bomb load. The protective covers are still in place on the pitot tube masts. No 149 Squadron was the fourth Bomber Command unit to be equipped with the Stirling.

A pair of No 218 Squadron aircraft make a low pass over either Marham or Downham Market sometime after mid-1942 when the Type C1 roundels and fin flash were introduced. The aircraft in the foreground is a Mk I Series III aircraft with a Frazer Nash FN7 dorsal turret. The aircraft in the background is either a late Mk I Series III or a Mk III with the late FN50 dorsal turret.

Stirling Mk II

During 1940 and 1941 plans were put into motion to have a number of British designed aircraft produced by the Canadian aircraft industry. Canadian production would be safe from enemy attack and the additional aircraft would be of great value to the war effort. During 1941, the Stirling was added to the production plan alongside the Lancaster and Mosquito. Initially the plan called for production of 140 aircraft which would be nearly identical to the Stirling Mk I. These aircraft differed from the Stirling Mk I in that they would be powered by American 1,600 hp Wright Cyclone R-2600-A5B radial engines, housed in redesigned cowlings. Under the Canadian production plan, all aircraft built in Canada with the American powerplants were to be designated Stirling Mk IIs.

A total of four aircraft were converted in England to use the American engines and two aircraft (N3657 and N3711) were test flown at Rochester in the Autumn of 1941. These tests revealed that the American engines gave no increase in performance and during early 1942 the entire Stirling Mk II production project was cancelled.

The Stirling Mk II prototype had revised engine cowlings to house the American built Wright Cyclone engines and had the upper carburetor air intakes deleted. The aircraft (N3657) never entered squadron service and was ultimately Struck Off Charge (SOC) on 16 September 1945.

The second Mk II prototype parked on the grass at Boscombe Down during March of 1942. The engine exhausts are located on the lower port side of the cowling. The Mk II project was cancelled and this aircraft (N3711), like the first prototype, never entered service and was retired on 30 November 1944.

Cowlings

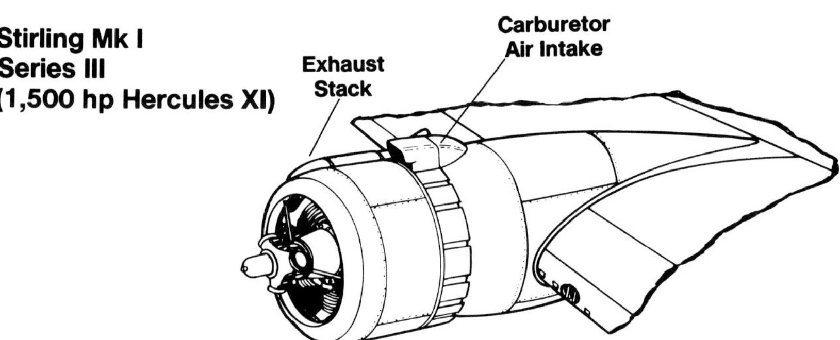

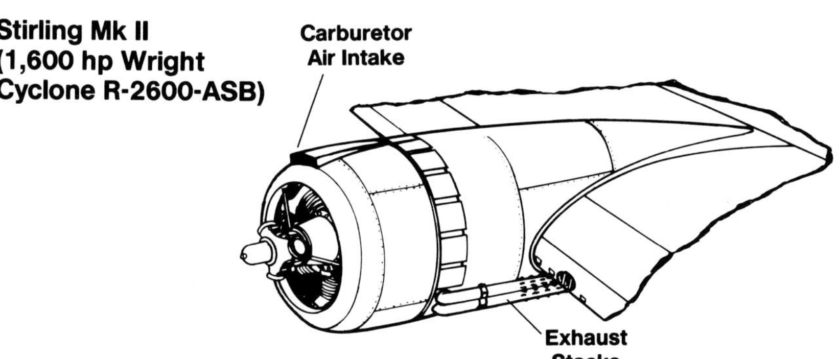

Stirling Mk III

During early 1942, Short decided to install more powerful engines in the Stirling in an effort to improve the aircraft's climb and ceiling. The engine selected was the 1,635 hp Hercules VI radial. The first of these engines arrived at Rochester and were installed in a Stirling Mk I (R9309) which was to serve as the prototype for the Stirling Mk III.

The Mk III differed external from the Mk I in the engine cowlings and fuselage window arrangement. To handle the more powerful Hercules VI engines, the cowlings were modified with the air intake on top of the cowling becoming longer and lower. The oil cooler was repositioned from the wing leading edge to a circular housing under the engine cowling just behind the cowl cooling gills. These oil coolers incorporated ice guards and air cleaners in the forward section of the housing while the cooling section was equipped with thermostatically controlled shutters.

The fuselage was modified with the number of fuselage windows being reduced. The port side of the fuselage now had a total of three windows forward and four windows behind the port main spar (although a fifth window just above the horizontal stabilizer was often installed). The starboard side of the fuselage now carried three windows forward and three behind the main spar. The nose windows on either side of the fuselage were modified with bulged blister type windows which improved visibility for the observer. This modification was particularly useful when picking out drop zones in Occupied Europe for the re-supply missions flown to support the Resistance movement.

Tests with R9303 at Boscombe Down during June of 1942 revealed that the initial rate of climb for the Mk III was 500 feet per minute. Between 12,000 and 15,000 feet, climb fell off to 300 feet per minute; however, this was a considerable improvement over the 160 feet per minute of the Mk I Series I aircraft. Maximum speed was 270 mph at 14,500 feet, some thirty-two mph faster than a Mk I Series I.

In September of 1942, R9303 suffered an inflight engine fire that forced the crew to abandon the aircraft. It was replaced by a second modified Mk I (R9188) and this aircraft was soon supplemented in the test program by the first pair of production Mk IIIs off the Austin Motors production line (BK648 and BK649). These aircraft were fitted with wire throttle controls replacing the earlier Exactor throttles; however, the modification did not cure the Stirling's throttle control difficulties.

Deliveries of the Stirling Mk III to service squadrons began during January 1943 with the third aircraft off the Austin Motors production line. The first squadron to receive the Mk III was No 15 Squadron and by the end of March no less than seventy-nine aircraft had been delivered to the seven operational Stirling units. Their arrival in combat coincided with an increase in Bomber Command activities.

All Stirling Mk IIIs left the production line fitted with the Frazer Nash FN 50A dorsal turret (which was also retrofitted to a number of earlier Mk I series III aircraft) in place of the earlier FN 7A turret. This turret was lower, offered far less drag that the earlier high turret and featured a clear canopy giving the gunner a clear view in all directions. During the first six months of 1943, a number of armament changes for the Stirling Mk III were proposed including installation of a Frazer Nash FN64 belly turret as well as replacing the FN20 rear turret with an FN82 turret armed with twin 50 caliber machine guns. These changes were not adopted as standard because of center of gravity problems, although a number of No 7 Squadron aircraft were fitted with the belly turret in place of the H2S radar. At one point it was proposed that the Mk III be fitted with a new B12 dorsal turret, but this proposal was abandoned.

Late Stirling Mk III had a number of minor modifications made to them, including application of smooth finish camouflage paint, improved sealing of the front turret, removal of the D/F loop antenna, and removal of the port pitot mast. Crew security in the event of a ditching was enhanced by the provision of individual K Type dinghies within the fuselage which supplemented the main J Type crew dinghy in the port wing compartment.

During the Autumn of 1943, the use of the Stirling as part of Main Force operations began to decline. A Bomber Command study of losses on raids to Nuremberg and Berlin between August and November of 1943 had shown that between ten and fifteen percent of the Stirlings committed were lost. This loss rate was much higher than either the Halifax or Lancaster. Part of the losses were credited to the deadly *Schrage Musik* form of underside attack made by German night-fighters.

As a counter to this, a 50 caliber machine was gun mounted in the rear escape hatch behind a perspex shield. This installation was successfully tested on a Stirling Mk III (EF466) at Rochester in August of 1943. Plans were made to modify a number of Stirling Mk IIIs with this mount as soon as possible and some were installed on aircraft assigned to Nos 149 and 199 Squadrons late in the year; however, by then the need for the gun had largely disappeared.

The Stirling unit assigned to 100 Group was No 199 Squadron, equipped with Stirling Mk IIIs. The squadron was based at North Creake from 1 May 1944 until March of 1945 when it converted to Halifaxes. The squadron specialized in dropping *Window*, strips of aluminum foil which were designed to jam German radar, to simulate a larger force of aircraft. Additionally the Stirlings were equipped with electronic radar jamming equipment known as *Mandrel*, which was able to jam sizeable sectors of the German early warning radar system. Sometimes such action was taken to cover an actual bomber force, while on other occasions the squadron was used to decoy German pilots into the air, exhausting both the pilots and their fuel supplies.

Externally, the Stirlings assigned to No 199 Squadron differed from standard Mk III bombers by the installation of a series of post antennas installed along the undersides of the fuselage for the *Mandrel* equipment and the rectangular chutes near the navigator's

The crew conducts engine run ups on a Stirling Mk III (EF465) of No 75 (New Zealand) Squadron, while the aircraft is chocked on the grass at Mepal. The Mk III had a revised cowling with an enlarged air intake and longer barbed exhausts. EF465 was listed as missing on 23/24 August 1943 on a mission against Berlin.

position (or just behind the fuselage bomb bay) for the bundles of *WINDOW*. The bulky *Mandrel* equipment was installed on the starboard side in the central fuselage and just behind the wireless operator's position with the operator facing the equipment.

The first Stirling *Mandrel* mission took place on the eve of D-Day (5 June 1944). The powerful transmissions from the *Mandrel* set, however, interfered with Allied aerial navigation and ground radio signals. Fortunately, future operations were to take place over the North Sea, cutting out interference.

A Stirling Mk III (EH957) of No 1654 Heavy Conversion Unit takes off on a training mission from Glatton Airfield, a USAAF B-17 base, during the Winter of 1944/45. This aircraft was later retired from active service on 28 March 1946.

Four Stirling Mk III fuselages on the production line await installation of various internal components, while three Frazer Nash turrets (nose, upper and tail) are positioned for mounting on their allotted airframe. A total of 2,368 Stirlings were produced.

Cowlings

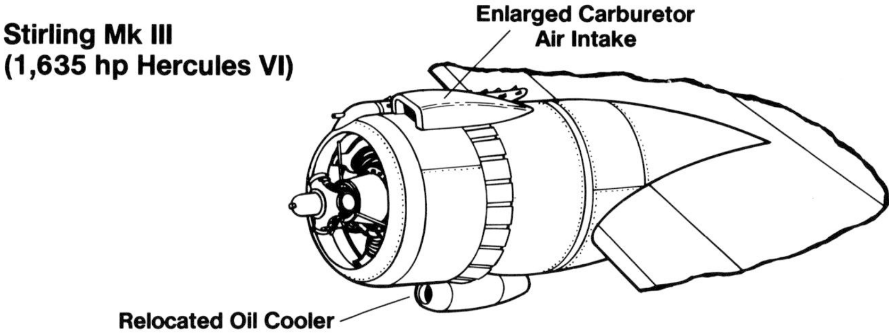

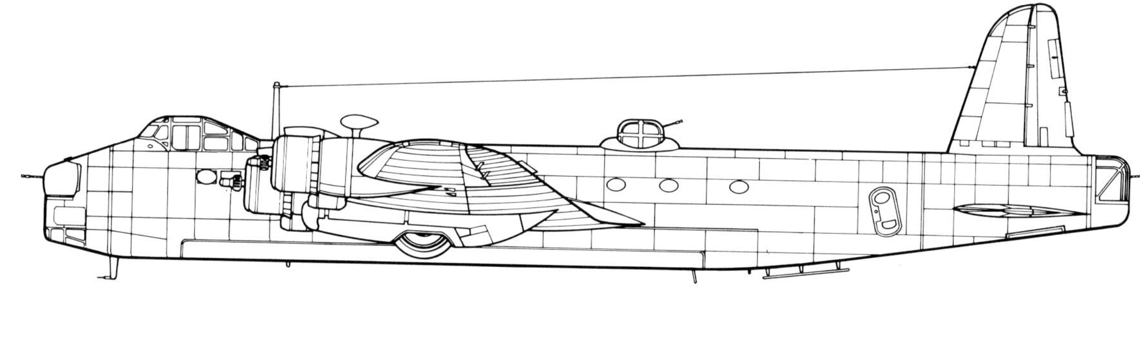

Specifications

Short Stirling Mk III

Wingspan .... 99 feet 1 inch
Length .... 87 feet 3 inches
Height .... 22 feet 9 inches
Empty Weight .... 46,900 pounds
Maximum Weight .... 70,000 pounds
Powerplants .... Four 1,635 hp Bristol Hercules VI or XVI air cooled radial engines.

Armament .... Nine .303 Browning machine guns in nose turret (2), dorsal turret (2), tail turret (4) and underfuselage hand held mount (1).
17,000 pounds of bombs

Performance

Maximum Speed .... 270 mph
Service ceiling .... 16,500 feet (maximum load)
Range .... 2,330 miles
Crew .... Seven

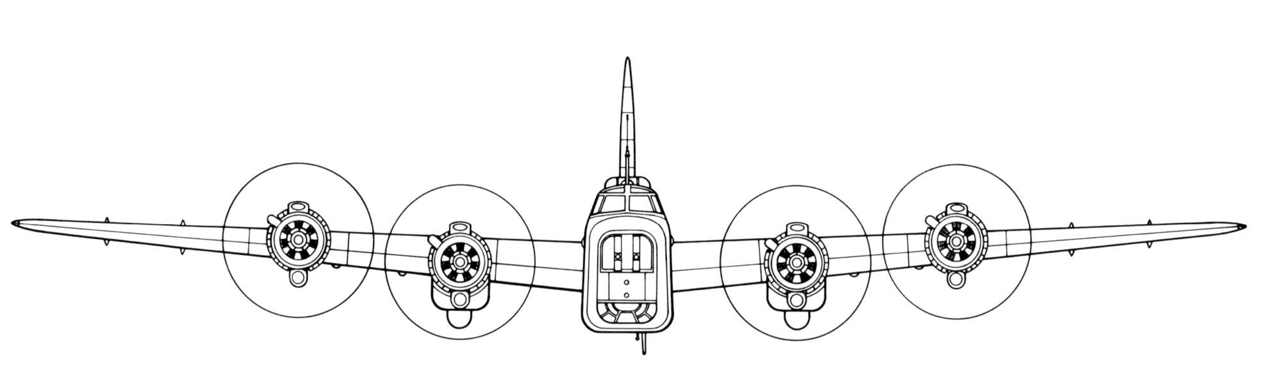

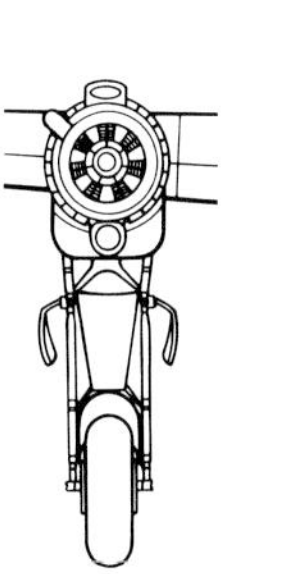

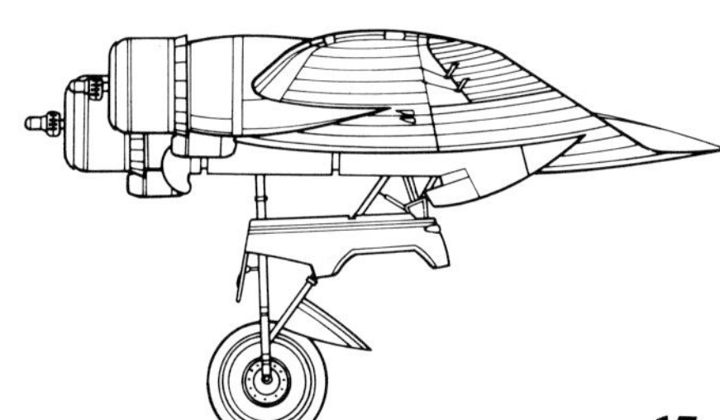

SGT Falconbridge of No 90 Squadron mans the FN50 upper turret on a Stirling Mk III. The fairing in front of the turret prevented the gunner from firing his weapons into the fuselage of his own aircraft. The FN50 turret replaced the earlier taller FN7 turret carried by Stirling Mk I Series III aircraft.

An RAF gunner mans the Frazer Nash rear turret of a Stirling. The ammunition belts were fed to the guns over rollers at the top of angled frames, which led to jams if the ammunition belts were out of alignment. The gun barrels of the four .303 machine guns were mounted in a staggered position.

Turrets

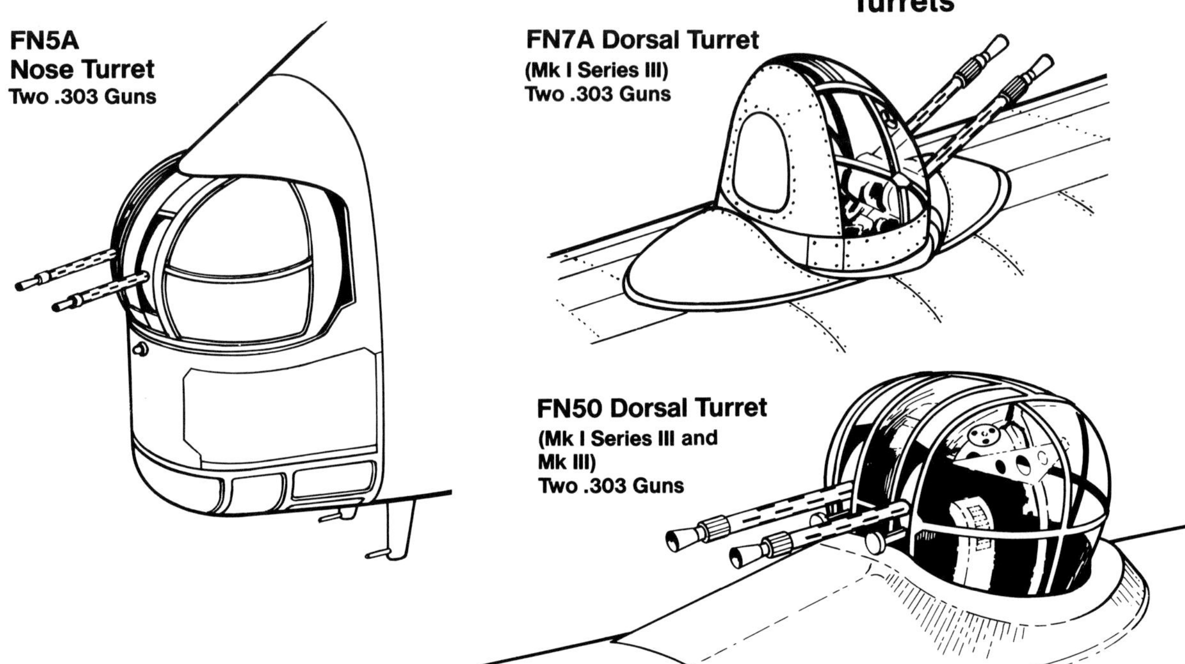

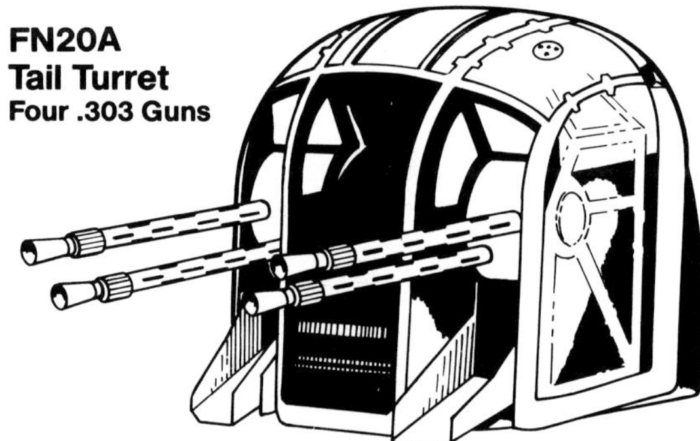

Retractable Belly Turret
(Mk I Series I Only)
Two .303 Guns

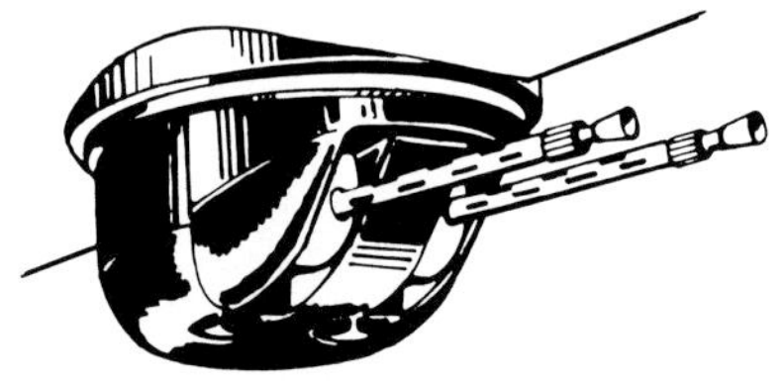

JOLLY ROGER **also carried a single pitot tube mast under the nose and a bulged blister type nose observation window. The forward *Mandrel* antenna mast is located on the underside of the nose behind the pitot tube mast.**

JOLLY ROGER**, a Stirling Mk III (R - Roger, LJ525) of No 199 Squadron, is parked on her dispersal spot at North Creake. This Stirling was equipped with *Mandrel* electronic countermeasures equipment and was fitted with a ventral machine gun mounting (directly under the X aircraft code letter).**

Mandrel Antennas

Stirling Mk III *Mandrel*

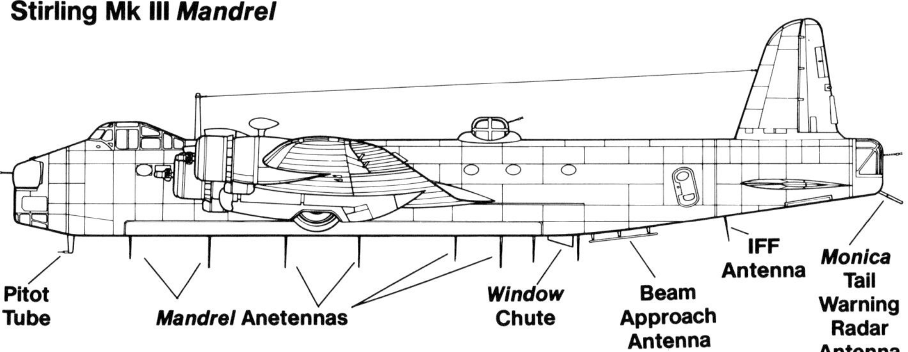

Many Mk IIIs served with Heavy Conversion Units (HCU) such as this Mk III of No 1651 HCU. The unit was first based at Wratting Common before moving to Woolfox Lodge. Training duties were sometimes supplemented by active operations such as diversionary sweeps to assist the main bomber force. No 1651 HCU used Stirlings until the end of 1944 when it converted to Lancasters.

Operations

All aircraft delivered to No 7 Squadron were built at Short's Rochester plant, and, as the Series III aircraft began arriving in the Squadron, pressure began to mount for the unit to begin offensive operations.

The pressure to begin operations, even though No 7 Squadron had only a handful of the operational Series III aircraft, came directly from the Prime Minister, Winston Churchill. With his eye for military drama, he had suggested that the squadron bomb Berlin as its first operational mission. Luckily, a more reasonable target was selected for the Stirling's first mission, the oil storage tanks at Rotterdam, Holland. Despite the presence of Series III aircraft at Oakington, the Stirlings dispatched early in the evening of 10 February 1941 were all Series I aircraft, each of which carried 8,000 pounds of bombs. The mission was a success and all aircraft returned safely to base.

The number of Stirlings serving within Bomber Command at any one time was never substantial. During the first twelve months of active operations, only three squadrons operated Stirlings. As the first Stirling unit, No 7 Squadron opened night operations with as many aircraft as their limited strength would allow.

During the Spring of 1942, the squadron moved to RAF Newmarket because of the muddy conditions at Oakington. In the initial weeks of operations from Newmarket, there were a number of belly landings caused by failures of the undercarriage motors which caused the gear to jam in the retracted position.

A second squadron joined No 7 Squadron, when No 15 Squadron converted to the Short bomber in April of 1941. These two squadrons made up the operational Stirling force until December of 1941, when No 18 Squadron was re-equipped with Stirlings. with Stirlings.

On the production side, Austin Motors had begun production of the Stirling Mk I, and tests at Boscombe Down with the first aircraft from the production line (W7426) reported that the elevator and aileron controls of the Austin Motors-built aircraft compared unfavorably with Short built machines; otherwise, the aircraft was acceptable.

The Stirling began daylight operations during April of 1941, mostly in the anti-shipping role. Night operations still involved the occasional attempted mission to Berlin, although the majority these sorties were aborted due to either bad weather and mechanical problems. The first Stirling loss to enemy action came on the night of 9/10 April when N6011 of No 7 Squadron, on a mission against Berlin, was intercepted and shot down near Lingen by a Bf 110 flown by *Feldwebel* Scherling of 7/NJG 1.

Beginning on 1 July 1941, Stirlings of No 3 Group were ordered to take part in *CIRCUS* operations over Northern France. These operations were designed to relieve some of the pressure on the Russians by drawing away Luftwaffe units from the Eastern Front. In the event, the two fighter *Geschwadern*, JG 2 and JG 26, stationed along the Channel proved more than capable of countering RAF incursions and no Luftwaffe units were diverted from the East.

Stirling losses during this period included one unfortunate aircraft which was downed by friendly fire. On 8 July, N6034 of No 7 Squadron was returning from a mission when it was shot down by British gunners. Occasionally, a Stirling was lost to enemy fighters while engaged on an anti-shipping mission. On 18 July, N6030 was attacked by a Bf 109F flown by *Feldwebel* Jackel of JG 26 over the English Channel. The Stirling's sturdy structure held up to six passes by the Messerschmitt — but not the seventh.

The presence of the SCHARNHORST, GNEISENAU, and PRINZ EUGEN in the French port of Brest prompted a number of sorties by Bomber Command in the hopes of incapacitating the ships. On 23 July, SCHARNHORST moved south to La Pallice and that same evening, an attack involving six Stirlings armed with 2,000 pound armor piercing bombs was launched. One aircraft was reported missing; however, the Stirlings had scored one hit on the battlecruiser. One successful and one aborted attack was mounted the following October and this pattern was repeated during December. The last attack came on 18 December when seventeen aircraft made a joint raid with Halifax and Manchester bombers. Flying at 14,000 feet, the Stirlings were well within flak range and also suffered from repeated fighter attacks. Of the seventeen Stirlings dispatched, four were lost.

During 1941, Bomber Command diversified its long range missions to include targets in Northern Italy. These targets lay beyond the Alps, and it was virtually impossible for the Stirling to maintain altitude with a full load and clear the mountain peaks. Crews reported that it was not uncommon to find Stirlings threading their way along valleys and passes in order to reach their objectives.

During 1942, Bomber Command, to aid the bomber force in achieving much needed bombing precision, formed an advance force of aircraft to go in ahead of the Main Force and illuminate the target area with marker flares. No 8 Path Finder Force (PFF) Group was established to perform this mission. Air Chief Marshall "Butch" Harris initially opposed the Path Finder Force plan because he thought that his best crews would be transferred from Main Force units, lowering the operational quality of his frontline units. In the event, his fears were to prove groundless.

The four PPF squadrons in Bomber Command were each equipped with the four operational bombers types flown by the Command and it was No 7 Squadron that formed the Stirling element of the PPF. The principle of target marking had previously been tried by No 3 Group. During the 1,000 bomber Cologne raid, No 15 Squadron had shared this duty with several other units. These sorties, however, had involved illuminating the target with incendiaries rather than flares. While both methods had shortcomings, the incendiary method depended upon ignition of ground objects. Flares, on the other and, were triggered in mid-air and allowed much closer spacing between the PFF units and Main Force. This also made the PPF units less vulnerable to the enemy's defenses.

There were never enough Stirlings available at any one time to mount regular missions of 100 or more aircraft. Despite the emphasis on night attacks, Stirlings still made occasional daylight sorties, mostly against U-Boat facilities in the Baltic. The U-Boat War was in a critical stage for the Allies and any effort by Bomber Command to slow U-boat production was welcomed by the Admiralty. Two Stirling raids on 16 and 19 July to the ports of Lubeck and Stettin, had the bombers taking-off and crossing the North Sea

This Stirling Mk I, A - Able, belongs to No 1657 Heavy Conversion Unit based at Stradishall, Suffolk. At one time the demands for trained crews led to the formation of at least eight Stirling Heavy Conversion Units (HCU).

Ground crewmen hoist 500 pound bombs, fitted with extended nose fuzes, into a Stirling Mk I of No 7 Squadron. The pitot tube mast covers are still in place. A number of aircraft were lost due to failure to remove these covers before take off. With the covers in place, the pilot had no way of knowing his airspeed.

during daylight, with their arrival over the target being timed for the onset of dusk. Few of the aircraft reached the first target and an absence of protective cloud cover on 19 July caused the bombers to divert to their secondary target of Vegesack on the Weser river.

Experience gained on daylight operational missions highlighted a problem with early Stirlings. The hydraulic lines that fed power to the dorsal and rear turrets were prone to battle damage from enemy beam attacks. The recuperators, which smoothed out the pulsations in the hydraulic power fed to the nose and dorsal turrets, were located immediately behind the bulls-eye of the fuselage roundel. After it was realized that the Germans had examined crashed Stirlings and were telling their fighter pilots to direct their fire into that region, the recuperators were immediately relocated to a less vulnerable area.

Tactical tests conducted by the Air Fighting Development Unit (AFDU) at Duxford in September had confirmed that the Stirling's turrets provided a good protection against beam and high angle attacks; however, the absence of an underside gun turret left the aircraft vulnerable to attacks from below. Until August of 1942, the dorsal turret installed on the Stirling Mk I was the Frazer Nash FN7A, an egg shaped unit with the rear section blanked over. After August of 1942, Mk Is began replacing this turret with an improved Frazer Nash FN50, which was also installed on the Stirling Mk III. These turrets were equipped with an interrupter gear which kept the gunner from firing into the wings or fuselage of his own aircraft. The gear was mounted on the fuselage and covered by a curved fairing on the front and rear of the turret base. The disadvantage of the FN50 turret, was that in order to bail out, the gunner had to leave the turret and escape through one of the fuselage hatches. The FN7A turret had its escape hatch incorporated into the turret's solid rear section.

By late 1942, there were enough Stirlings on hand to meet operational needs and to establish two Heavy Conversion Units (HCU). These units allowed new Stirling aircrews to be given additional training in its systems and flying characteristics before arriving at an operational squadron. Many of the aircraft assigned to the HCUs, however, were "war weary", resulting in a high accident rate.

Bomber Command's primary function up to March of 1942, had been in the night bombing role. After March of 1942, the command received a secondary duty, of sowing sea mines along the main enemy shipping channels around the European coast. This secondary mission was to prove highly successful with a number of sinkings being credited to aerial mines over the next three years.

The Stirling proved to be particularly well suited for this role, with the standard 1,500 pound Type A Mk V mine being slim enough to fit into the aircraft's bomb bay. Mining operations were given the code name *Gardening* and were carried out primarily in Danish waters, where deep water channels linked the Baltic and North Seas. At first the mines were dropped from low level, with the danger of inadvertently flying into the water during release. Additionally, the presence of flak ships anchored in the channels at strategic positions led to a steady toll of the attacking Stirlings.

The invasion of North Africa in November of 1942 led to a return to targets in Northern Italy. During the raid on Turin on 28 November, the pilot of BF372 (OJ-H) of No 149 Squadron was so determined to identify the aiming point that he made three runs over the target. On the third run he was critically wounded, being hit in the eye, chest and leg. Despite his wounds, and with a freezing slipstream stabbing through the shattered windscreen, he flew the damaged Stirling back over the Alps. When he crossed the

King George VI climbs out of a Stirling Mk I (BF345) at RAF Stradishall, home of No 1657 Heavy Conversion Unit (HCU). The White stripe around the rear fuselage was a trainer identification marking. The White Danger warning marking informs personnel not to touch any switches or levers to avoid accidentally retraction of the undercarriage!

English coast, he ordered the crew to bail out. The front gunner (F/SGT Mackie) and flight engineer (F/SGT Jeffrey) volunteered to remain with their pilot, and all three were lost when the Stirling crashed into the English Channel. For his gallantry, F/SGT Rawdon Hume Middleton was posthumously awarded the Victoria Cross, Britain's highest military award.

The internal fuselage configuration of the Stirling was never basically altered. There was a central floor even with the top of the forty-two foot long bomb bay, with a step down into the bomb aimer's compartment in the nose and a similar step down into the aircraft's rear fuselage. The pilot's compartment was on a platform some two to three feet above the bomb bay floor. The main throttle levers were mounted on a console between the pilot's seats, and the control yokes were provided with large elliptical wheel grips. The navigator was positioned directly behind the port pilot's seat and the wireless operator sat behind him. The flight engineer's station was located behind the starboard pilot's position. This arrangement was suitable when Stirlings were flown by two pilots; however, when the crew complement was later reduced to one pilot, it meant that the engineer could not assist the pilot. Stirling pilots had to handle both the controls and throttles, while on the Halifax and Lancaster these duties were split between the pilot and engineer.

A definite physical advantage of the Stirling's internal layout was the absence of a main wing spar to obstruct crew movement. This advantage proved vital whenever a crew had to abandon the aircraft in a hurry. Another advantage was that the mid-upper gunner could quickly step into and out of his turret, unlike other British heavies.

The Stirling was provided with escape hatches in the nose, two located on the fuselage top between the cockpit and the dorsal turret, and another in the rear of the fuselage. Rear gunners could rotate their turrets and bail out backwards (after retrieving their parachutes from the fuselage). The top hatches were rarely used for bail outs, but were widely used during ditchings, because the dinghy (life raft) storage compartment was located in the port wing a few feet outboard of the fuselage.

With the introduction of the Stirling Mk III during January of 1943, squadron strength began to build and for the first time since its service introduction, the number of Stirlings available for raids reached up to and just beyond 100 aircraft per mission. Mk IIIs (as well earlier Mk Is) continued to fly mining missions and the original low level method of mine delivery was changed to a safer high level method, due to the success of tests conducted with a Stirling (BK594) of the Bombing Development Unit. This same aircraft was also tested with a variety of active and passive electronic devices including *Oboe*, *Boozer* and *Fishpond*, the latter pair being electronic warning equipment which warned crews of the presence of German night-fighters.

During July of 1943, the raids on the Ruhr industrial complexes were replaced by a series of missions against Germany's huge industrial and port complex at Hamburg. For many months, the British had debated the use of a radar jamming device, code named *WINDOW*. This consisted of aluminum foil strips which was scattered from the bombers, jamming German radars. It was particularly effective against the short range *Wurzburg* warning radars, creating a snowstorm effect on the operator's screen. German fire control/gun laying radar sets could also be jammed by the aluminum strips. Originally, the British delayed introducing *WINDOW* because of the possibility that the Germans would copy the material and use it against British defenses.

By mid-1943, the new American developed SCR700 airborne radar had been made available for use on British night-fighters. This radar had proven to be virtually immune to *WINDOW* jamming and Bomber Command was given clearance to utilize *WINDOW* over Germany. During its first use, radar controlled enemy searchlight, flak and night-fighter units were thrown into total, if temporary, confusion. Thanks to this confusion, the Lancasters, Halifaxes and Stirlings completed their mission with very small losses. A

A pair of 2,000 pound light case bombs are hoisted into the narrow bomb bay of a Stirling Mk I of No 7 Squadron. The narrow width of the bomb bays limited the carriage of high explosive bombs to those of no more than 2,000 pounds, since larger weapons were too wide to fit in the bay. The cases on the bomb trolleys contain incendiary clusters.

combination of dry weather and concentrated bombing created conditions during the second night raid (The 8th USAAF having bombed Hamburg during the day) for a fire storm. This fire storm killed some 50,000 people and gutted a large portion of the city.

The German defenses reacted more quickly to the threat from *WINDOW* than the British expected. It is likely, however, that the system of night-fighters orbiting specific zones under radar control was becoming too limited against the British bomber streams and the introduction of *WINDOW* only accelerated the change in Luftwaffe countermeasures. German tactics now placed the Me 110s and Ju 88s directly into the bomber stream, leaving target selection up to the night-fighter crews.

During August, a raid was launched against Peenemunde, the center for German rocket research projects. The bomber crews were not briefed as to the nature of their target but were told that raids would be scheduled against Peenemunde until the facility was destroyed — a chilling prospect considering that Peenemunde was located on the Baltic coast, well inside Germany! Fortunately, the attack launched on 17/18 August was thought to have so seriously damaged the facilities and caused so many key personnel casaualties, a repeat raid was unnecessary. This raid delayed the V-2 offensive on England by at least two months.

After Peenemunde, a series of operations were mounted against Italian targets, and Stirlings were a major component of the attacking force. During the Turin sortie of 12/13 August, a second and last Victoria Cross was earned by a Stirling crew member. The pilot of a No 218 Squadron Stirling, F/SGT Arthur Louis Aaron, was struck by a burst of fire from the rear guns of another Stirling. Wounded in the face and chest, Aaron was rendered unconscious for the bulk of the flight until the damaged aircraft was approaching the North African coast (the crew had decided to divert to Africa rather than try to climb back over the Alps).

R - Robert (W7513) of No 15 Squadron nosed over at the end of the runway on return from the second 1,000 bomber raid against Essen on 1/2 June 1942. The upper wing surfaces are streaked and scuffed by the ground crew's boots. The Stirling was repaired and later served with Nos 149 and 75 Squadrons before being declared missing on a mining mission over Kiel Bay on 29 April 1943.

A Stradishall based Stirling Mk I of 1657 Heavy Conversion Unit on a training flight over England. The tail wheels were often left down on non-operational flights to allow the rear gunner an unobstructed access into and out of his turret.

This Stirling Mk I (BK601) was one more victim of the Stirling's weak undercarriage. The aircraft had been on active service with Nos 214 and 149 Squadrons, before being assigned to No 1657 HCU. The aircraft was on a visit to the USAAF 94th Bomb Group base at Rougham on 28 January 1944, when the accident occurred.

As the aircraft approached the airfield at Bone, F/SGT Aaron insisted on getting back into the pilot's seat. Although unable to actually take over the controls, since one arm was almost severed, he attempted to assist the flight engineer and bomb-aimer, by lining up the Stirling for landing. Despite his help, the aircraft overshot the runway and had to abort the landing twice. The third attempt ended in what was virtually a controlled crash, although the crew survived. Unfortunately, F/SGT Aaron died of his wounds some nine hours later.

The last Main Force raid for the Stirling was on 22/23 November 1943, and the target was the same one that Churchill had called for when the aircraft made its operational debut — Berlin. After this raid, the remainder of Stirling missions within Bomber Command would be mine-laying, electronic countermeasures and agent/supply drops over Europe.

Up to early 1944, Bomber Command was forced to rely on either routing the Main Force to and from the target via an indirect route or on small elements of Mosquitoes dropping *Window* and flares over a selected area away from the primary target. These tactics all too often failed to prevent attacks by Me 110s and Ju 88s of the German *Nachtjadggeschwadern*. In the thirteen months between March 1943 and 1944, over 2,000 heavy bombers were declared as Missing In Action (MIA).

To counter German night defenses, a special unit was formed to conduct electronic countrmeasures missions. During January of 1944, the first units destined to form 100 Group arrived at Sculthorpe in North Norfolk. Within a few months 100 Group had Nos 214, 199, 223, and 462 Squadrons operating from the same region. 100 Group's motto was "Confound and Destroy" and using a mixture of active and passive devices such as *Window*, *Mandrel*, *Carpet* and *Jostle* the Group's aircraft would proceed the Main Force and either disrupt enemy radio and radar channels or act as a decoy. The Stirling unit assigned to 100 Group was No 199 Squadron flying modified Stirling Mk IIIs which carried *Mandrel* equipment. Their first mission was flown on 5 June 1944. No 199 Squadron operated the Stirling Mk III until March of 1945 when it converted to the Halifax.

A Stirling Mk I (N3705) from No 7 Squadron crash landed relatively undamaged in Holland on 16 August 1942 and was salvaged by the Luftwaffe. Luftwaffe personnel packed the buckled nose area with straw bales and a canvas cover was secured to the nose with webbing. The aircraft undersurfaces were repainted in Yellow.

N3705 taxies out on its delivery flight to the Rechlin Test Center, repainted in full German markings. The Yellow undersurface color extended about a third of the way up the fuselage sides. The escort aircraft for the delivery flight was a Ju 88.

A group of German officers watch as the ex-No 7 Squadron Stirling Mk I runs up its engines at Rechlin during September of 1942. The nose covering has been painted Black. The Germans used a number of captured aircraft as trainers to instruct their fighter pilots on the best ways to attack Allied bombers. (Stapfer)

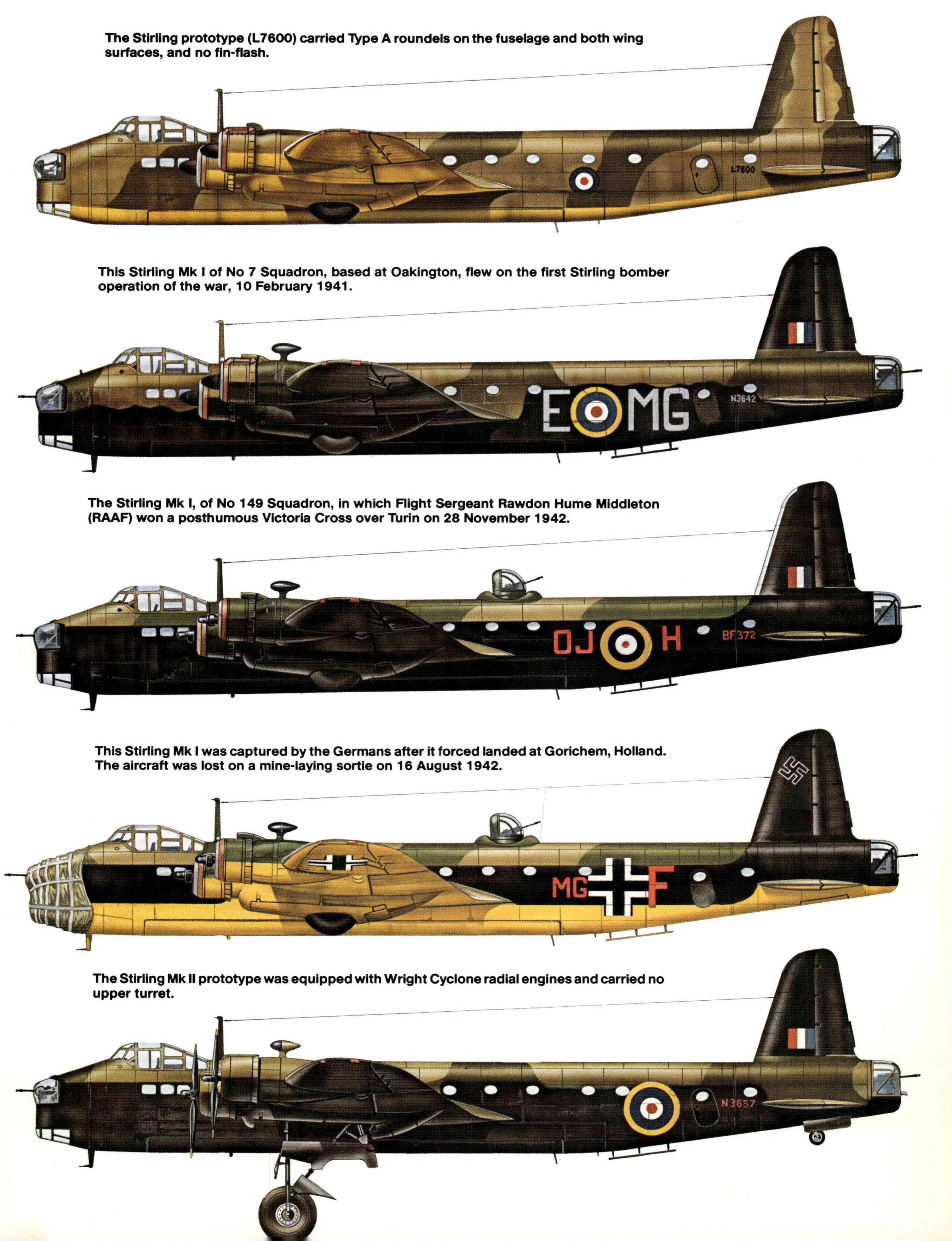

The Stirling prototype (L7600) carried Type A roundels on the fuselage and both wing surfaces, and no fin-flash.

This Stirling Mk I of No 7 Squadron, based at Oakington, flew on the first Stirling bomber operation of the war, 10 February 1941.

The Stirling Mk I, of No 149 Squadron, in which Flight Sergeant Rawdon Hume Middleton (RAAF) won a posthumous Victoria Cross over Turin on 28 November 1942.

This Stirling Mk I was captured by the Germans after it forced landed at Gorichem, Holland. The aircraft was lost on a mine-laying sortie on 16 August 1942.

The Stirling Mk II prototype was equipped with Wright Cyclone radial engines and carried no upper turret.

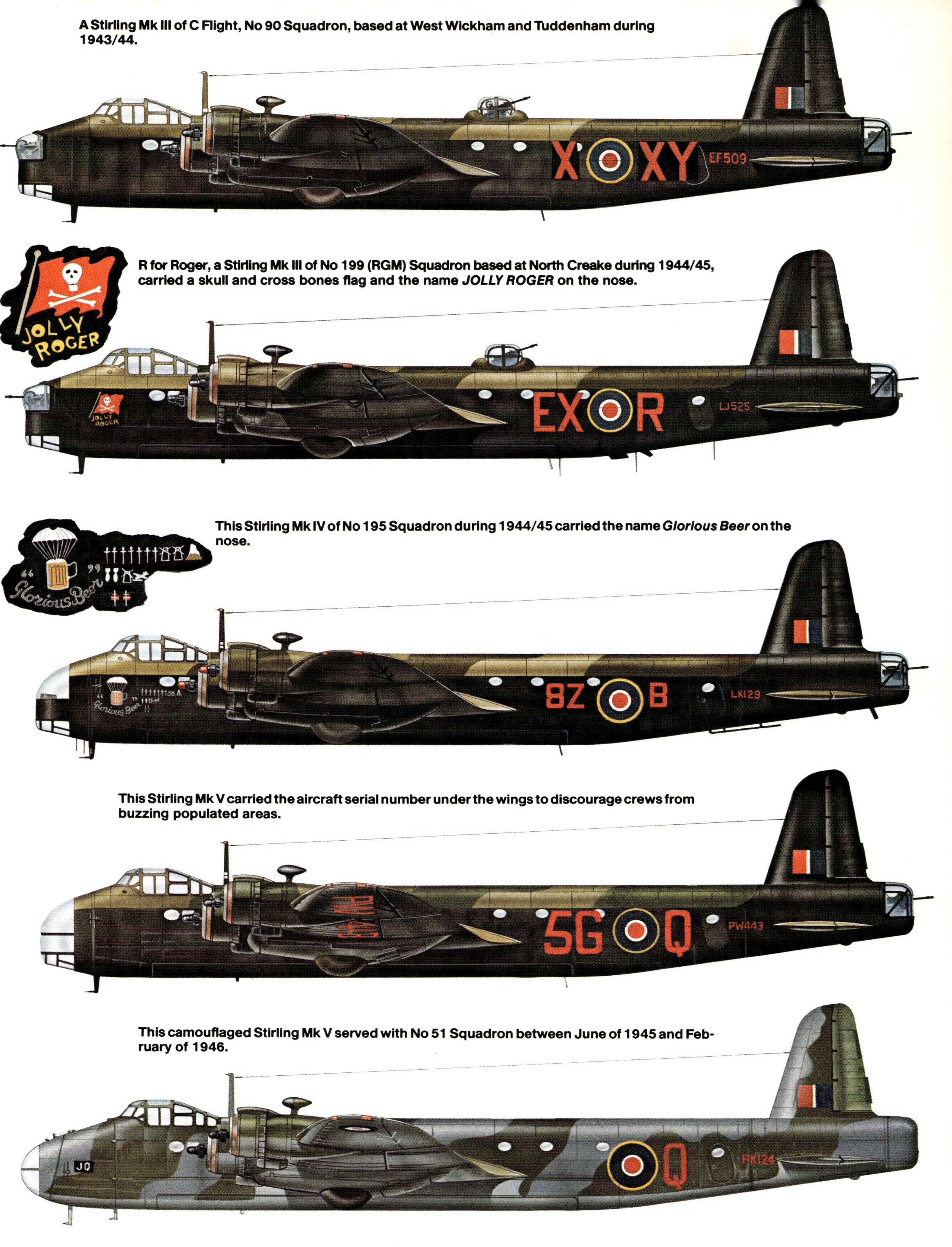

A Stirling Mk III of C Flight, No 90 Squadron, based at West Wickham and Tuddenham during 1943/44.

R for Roger, a Stirling Mk III of No 199 (RGM) Squadron based at North Creake during 1944/45, carried a skull and cross bones flag and the name *JOLLY ROGER* on the nose.

This Stirling Mk IV of No 195 Squadron during 1944/45 carried the name *Glorious Beer* on the nose.

This Stirling Mk V carried the aircraft serial number under the wings to discourage crews from buzzing populated areas.

This camouflaged Stirling Mk V served with No 51 Squadron between June of 1945 and February of 1946.

The flight engineer's station was equipped with a large main instrument panel. The circular valve controls for supercharger, carburetor, fuel tank and cabin heating regulation are behind the flight engineer's seat and extended to the port side of aircraft.

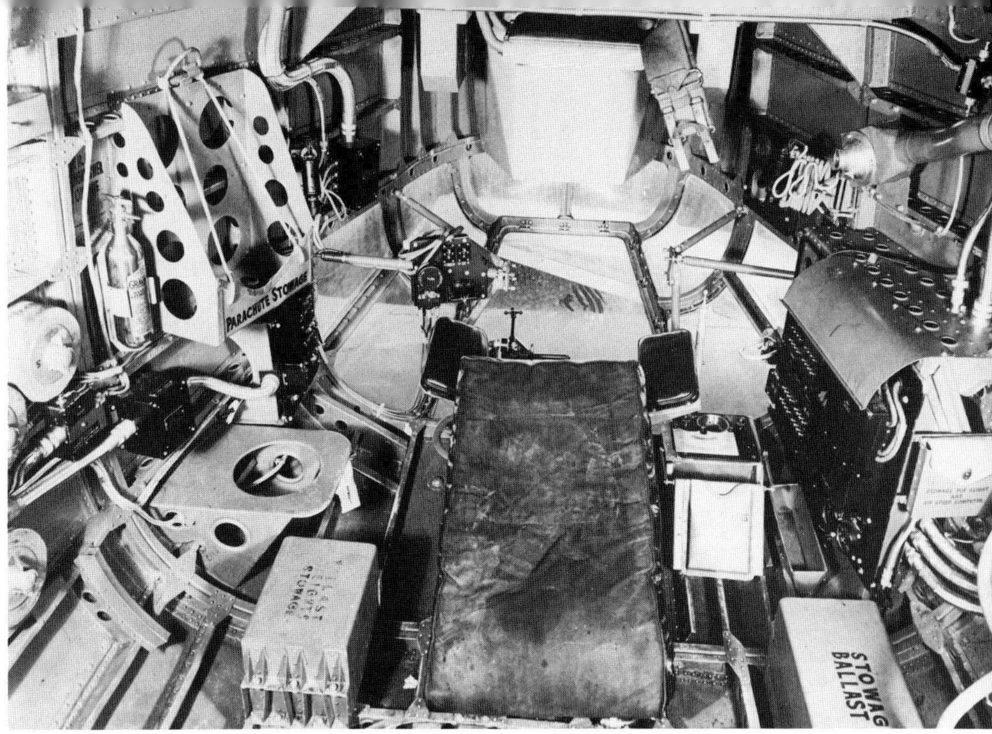

The Bomb-aimer's compartment was dominated by the flat optical bomb aiming panel in the nose. the main control box for the various functions of bomb fuse setting, bomb release and bomb bay door operation was on the starboard side, while a parachute stowage box was mounted on the port side.

A Stirling Mk III (BK784) of No 90 Squadron rests on her dispersal parking spot at Tuddenham. The aircraft's mission tally is carried on the fuselage side just behind the crew access door in White. This Stirling later crashed at Chippenham Lodge on 23 May 1944 after it swung on takeoff and hit a tree.

Ground crewmen perform maintenance on a the starboard outboard engine of a Stirling Mk I. The three square protruding shapes on the wing leading edge are barrage balloon cable cutters, while the circular intake in the wing leading edge is the oil cooler intake.

A number of Stirlings carried nose art. ***THE GREMLIN TEASER*** **was a Mk III (LJ542) of No 199 Squadron which carried the individual side code letter G. She was later Stricken Off Charge (SOC, i.e. retired from service) on 31 January 1945.**

Another No 199 Squadron Stirling Mk III with nose art was B - Beer (LJ560) which had a bear holding a beer bottle painted on the nose. The mission symbols carried by B - Beer were small foaming beer mugs. The Stirling was heavily damaged after the undercarriage collapsed on landing on 29 August 1944.

A Stirling Mk I undergoes undercarriage retraction tests while safely up on jack stands. The two stage undercarriage first retracted upwards, than forward to rest in the wheel well. The main wheel remained partially exposed when the undercarriage was fully retracted.

These early Mk Is Series III aircraft are assigned to No 15 Squadron at Wyton. The aircraft in the foreground appears to have had the pitot tubes removed from the under nose twin pitot masts and replaced by a single pitot tube mounted on the radio mast. The main wheel tires are covered to prevent dripping oil from damaging the tires.

A Stirling Mk III of an unknown squadron on final approach, moments before touch down. The enlarged upper cowling air intakes are visible as are the twin tail wheels.

D - Dog of No 218 (Gold Coast) Squadron displays seventeen mission symbols in White on the side of the nose along with a Dumbo cartoon character. The port inboard engine was equipped with twin hydraulic pumps which provided power to the nose and dorsal turrets, while a third hydraulic pump on the starboard inboard engine provided power for the rear turret.

An aircrew prepares to board a Stirling Mk III of No 199 Squadron at Lakenheath during 1944. The wing surfaces are streaked with oil thrown back by the engines and the light areas on the wing upper surface are engine exhaust strains. The absence of heavy flight clothing suggests that this is to be a non-operational flight.

Pilot Officer Peter Buck (Royal New Zealand Air Force, left) inspects the damage to the tail turret and rudder of his Stirling Mk III of No 75 (New Zealand) Squadron. The perspex turret center section was completely shot away by enemy fire over Essen and the escape hatch cover just forward of the turret was jettisoned.

B-17Fs of the 381st BG (533rd and 534th Bomb Squadrons) moved into Ridgewell in June of 1943; however, No 90 Squadron's Stirlings did not finally transfer out until after the Americans were well established. The last No 90 Squadron Stirling lifts off on its departure flight from the field, enroute to its new home base.

This Stirling Mk III (LJ569) of No 199 Squadron crashed during takeoff from North Creake on 15 September 1944. The starboard wing was torn off inboard of the engine and is visible just under the fuselage. Not surprisingly, C - Charlie was declared fit only for the scrap heap.

This Stirling Mk III (LK437) of No 1657 HCU lost power during a forced landing to Ridgewell on 15 November 1944 and came down short of the runway. The crew were fortunate to survive the crash with only minor injuries.

Stirling Mk IV

The value of paratroop and glider borne forces during the Second World War had been demonstrated by the German *Fallschirmjager* during 1940/41, and a similar use of airborne forces was recognized by the Allies to be vital to a successful invasion of Europe. The Douglas C-47 transport was perfect for carrying paratroops and their personal weapons, but neither the British nor the Americans had an aircraft which could tow the large British Horsa and Hamilcar gliders. These large gliders were capable of transporting support equipment ranging from light caliber guns to light tanks, equipment which was vital to the lightly armed paratroops.

To tow these large gliders, a four engined aircraft was urgently required; however, none could be spared from operations over Europe or the Atlantic until 1943. The Stirling had been designed with troop transport in mind as a secondary mission, but the small doors in the fuselage sides could not handle high exit rates required to keep the paratroops from spreading out too far. Despite this handicap, Stirlings were occasionally used for dropping small paratroop forces on special missions.

In the Stirling, the British recognized that they had an aircraft with the necessary power to tow the large gliders, and trials were begun to determine if the Stirling could be modified to serve as a glider tug. Glider towing trials were made with a Stirling Mk III (BK645) in April of 1943 and proved the feasibility of using the Stirling as a tow aircraft. With the successful completion of these tests, it was decided to convert a number of early Stirlings to the glider towing role under the designation Stirling Mk IV.

To improve the Stirling's performance in the glider towing role, the front and dorsal turrets were deleted, with the nose turret opening being faired over with a clear Perspex nose cone. The glider towing equipment was mounted on a yoke around the rear fuselage just behind the horizontal stabilizers. To save weight, the internal fuel load was reduced from the normal 2,254 gallons to 1,165 gallons. Even with this reduced fuel capacity, all potential drop zones in Western Europe remained within the Stirling's range.

By mid-1943, Short had produced plans for three Stirling transport variants. The "A" plan called for the conversion of Stirling Mk IIIs to the Mk IVs glider tug configuration. Plan "B" called for new production Stirling Mk IVs, while Plan "C" called for a redesign of the Stirling fuselage for freight and cargo under the designation Stirling Mk V.

Tests with the first two Stirling Mk IV conversions (EF503 and EF506) revealed that at a maximum weight of 70,000 pounds, the Stirling Mk IV had a ceiling of 19,000 feet and an estimated range of 2,360 miles at 10,000 feet (2,245 gallon of fuel on board). In order to prevent the engines from over heating when towing heavy loaded gliders, the engines were fitted with cooling fans and propeller spinners. A number of Stirling bomber Mk IIIs were converted to the Mk IV configuration, followed by the first production Mk IV (EF317) which rolled off the assembly line during December of 1943.

In addition to towing gliders the Mk IV also was envisioned as a paratroop transport and a number were modified with a large exit hatch installed in the fuselage underside just behind the bomb bay. These aircraft also had a retractable steel frame mounted under the rear fuselage to prevent the metal parachute strops from damaging the fuselage sides. A number of these aircraft also had the rear turret removed and the opening faired over with a clear Perspex cover. Production Stirling Mk IVs also had the twin pitot tube masts under the nose replaced by a single mast.

Between January and July of 1944, some six squadrons received the Stirling Mk IV, all six units being incorporated into No 38 Group. During this time period the units performed training missions in the techniques of glider towing in preparation for the invasion of Europe, as well as active missions to drop agents and supplies to the Resistance.

This Mk III (LK403) of No 196 Squadron is fitted with a glider towing yoke installed under the rear turret as part of the tests conducted to determine if the Stirling could tow large gliders. The tests were successful and led to the Stirling Mk IV. This Stirling later ended its career at No 1665 HCU where it was written off after it crashed when the undercarriage failed.

Nose Development

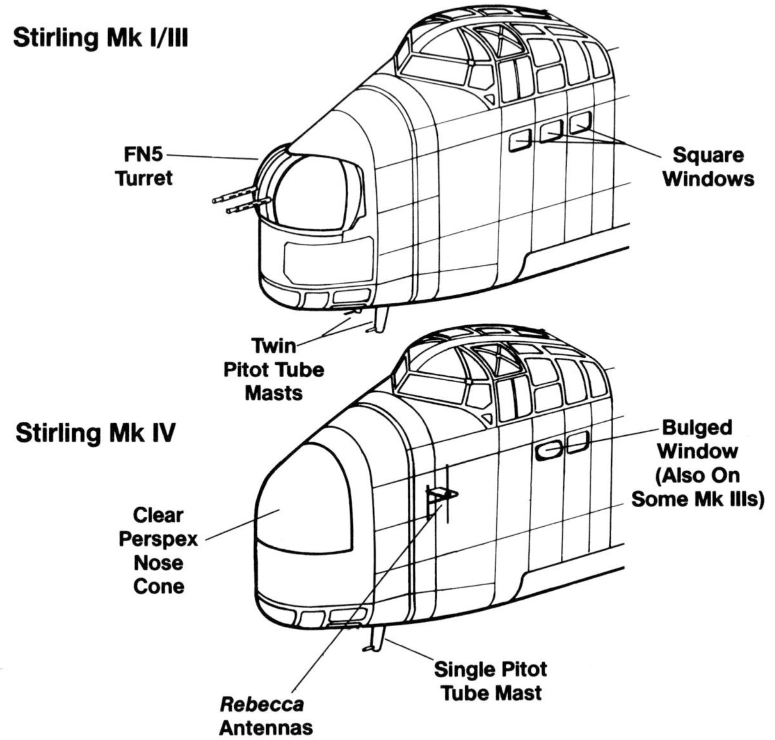

D-Day

On the night of 5/6 June, Stirlings of Nos 190, 196, 299, and 620 Squadrons took off from airfields west of London as part of the first wave of the D-Day invasion force. These Stirlings dropped the men of the British 6th Airborne Division around the vital bridges over the Orne and Caen Canals. The paratroops would seize and hold the bridges until relieved by advancing ground forces from the nearby Normandy beaches.

The following afternoon and evening, Stirlings towed some seventy Horsa gliders packed with men and equipment to reinforce the paratroop units. As a visual aid to friendly ground and air force units, the Stirlings were marked with standard D-Day recognition markings, consisting of three White and two Black bands painted around the rear fuselage and outboard wing sections. All aircraft involved in the D-Day Invasion carried these markings (except high-level four-engined bombers).

Arnhem

On the evening of 16 September 1944, the operational strength of No 38 Group stood at approximately 112 Stirling Mk IVs in six squadrons. The following day, this entire force took off, bearing paratroops and towing gliders loaded with the men and equipment of the 1st British Airborne Division, the famous "Red Devils."

Their objective was a small Dutch town on the border with Germany, whose bridge over the Rhine was the focal point for Operation MARKET GARDEN. This daring but risky plan was designed to force a corridor up though Holland and over the Rhine. Once secure, the corridor would be used by the British 2nd Army to advance into Germany and encircle the industrial centers of the Ruhr valley. American paratroops were equally involved, successfully securing a series of bridges at Eindhoven, Grave and Nijmegen; however, their success would be wasted without taking the bridge at Arnhem.

The initial drops went off almost without resistance both on the ground and in the air. The drop zones, however, were some seven miles from the bridge and unknown to the "Red Devils,' an unreported Panzer Division was in a position to block their advance. Within twenty-four hours, the Germans counter-attacked and brought in additional anti-aircraft weapons to halt the aerial resupply effort. The advance of the relieving force to the South was held up by stubborn German resistance and the original plan to seize the Arnhem bridge within forty-eight hours, the maximum time the lightly equipped Airborne troops were expected to hold, fell apart. The battle was to last almost a week, with the paratroops being pushed into a steadily shrinking pocket.

The Stirling squadrons supporting the paratroops paid a heavy price in aircraft and crews. No less than ten Stirling Mk IVs were listed as missing on the 19th, eleven were lost the following day and one out of every seven dispatched went down on the 21st. Tragically, the bulk of the supplies dropped fell into German hands, mainly due to the failure of the ground radio sets to transmit at a range that would allow the Stirling crews to accurately determine the paratroops' positions. By the time the last resupply operation was flown on 24 September, No 38 Group had lost some sixty-three Mk IVs, over half the number committed to action.

Rhine Crossing

As the Allies prepared for the push into the German heartland, they began planning for Operation VARSITY, a combined airborne and waterborne assault across the Rhine river. On 24 March, Stirling Mk IVs of No 38 Group left England towing some 143 Horsa gliders bearing the men and equipment of the British 6th Airborne Division. Six landing zones had been designated around the town of Hammenkiln, and thanks to almost perfect weather conditions, the vast majority of the gliders successfully landed in their allotted zones. Ground defenses had been partially taken out by fighter-bombers of the 2nd Tactical Air Force and glider losses were fortunately low. By the end of the day, British Army units had crossed the Rhine and were in defensive positions on the east bank.

One of the two Mk IIIs (EF506) which served as prototypes for the Stirling Mk IV conversion has had the mid-upper turret position faired over and the nose turret replaced by an unframed perspex cover. The device under the nose just behind the pitot tube masts is a test camera installation. This Stirling did not enter front line service and was SOC on 5 June 1945.

A finger four formation of Stirling Mk IVs of No 620 Squadron still painted with their D-Day fuselage invasion stripes. The painted out D-Day stripes on the wing uppersurfaces indicates this mission was flown after August of 1944. The small size of the Squadron code letters painted on the fuselage side was a normal practice for No 620 Squadron.

This Stirling Mk IV has just dropped a supply container from the under fuselage six foot by three foot hatch. The strop guard on the tail is in its lowered position to protect the fuselage from damage.

Besides these three major airborne operations, the Stirling Mk IV squadrons flew countless other sorties. Some of these involved ferrying aviation fuel to the forward airfields used by Allied fighter squadrons, while others involved dropping of Special Air Service elite units behind enemy lines. The majority of sorties, however, concerned SOE (Special Operations Executive) duties. These flights usually involved aircraft dispatched singly, at night and at low level. Once the enemy coast was crossed, the bomb-aimer would move from the co-pilot's seat, where he had assisted the pilot by handling the throttles, into the nose. From this position, he would navigate the aircraft along a predetermined course to the drop-zone and back to the coast.

Over the drop-zone a prearranged signal was flashed to the Stirling crew, without which, the drop would be cancelled. The supply containers were usually carried in the bomb bays; however, occasionally the Stirlings would carry supply baskets which were released through the rear, under fuselage hatch by either the flight engineer or wireless operator.

One of the last missions for the Stirling Mk IV was the pleasant task of bringing home British POWs. The majority of flights were made from Brussels where these unfortunate personnel had been assembled from the various POW camps throughout Germany. During 1945, a similar service was performed for servicemen returning to England for demobilisation. By March of 1946 most Stirling squadrons had either been disbanded or had converted to other aircraft and the last Stirling Mk IV was retired from RAF service.

Glider Yoke And Strop Guard

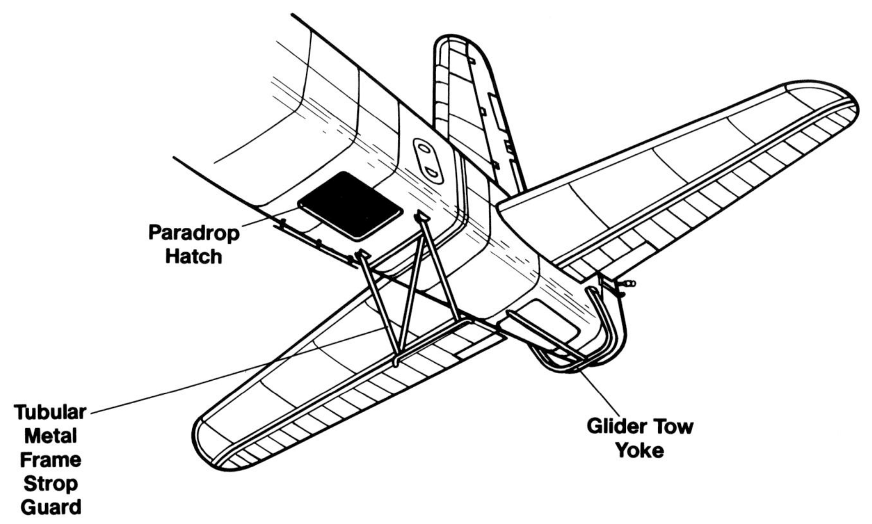

Stirling Mk IVs of an unidentified squadron line up on the taxiway of a British airfield just prior to commencing D-Day operations. The Black and White invasion markings were carried by all Allied aircraft involved with D-Day except four-engined strategic bombers.

Five Stirling Mk IVs of an unidentified squadron tow Horsa gliders across the English Channel on the afternoon of D-Day (6 June 44) to reinforce British paratroop forces holding positions beyond the Allied beachheads.

A Stirling Mk IV tows a Horsa glider enroute to Arnham, Holland on 17 September 1944. Stirlings of No 38 Group provided much of the aerial resupply effort at Arnham. The glider in the background is a Hamilcar.

(Below) Paratroopers of the British 1st Airborne Division wait to board Horsa gliders which will be towed by Stirling Mk IVs of No 620 Squadron on the morning of 17 September 1944. Within nine days, the majority of these men would either be dead or POWs following the unsuccessful attempt to secure the Arnhem bridge.

(Above) Stirling Mk IVs wait their turn to be attached to Horsa gliders as another Horsa begins its takeoff run. The SGTS in the foreground are believed to be from the Glider Regiment. The recessed door on the Horsa is the personnel entrance door.

This Mk IV of No 190 Squadron was one of the casualties of the Arnhem operations on 21 September 1944. The aircraft lost its port wing in the crash landing and the side canopy of the rear turret appears to have been damaged by enemy fire.

This Stirling Mk IV was just assigned to No 148 Squadron at Brindisi, Italy, and had the unit FS squadron code letters applied when it and the Halifax Mk Vs in the background were replaced by American built B-24 Liberators.

This Stirling MK IV of No 570 Squadron has the early Perspex nose cap and carries under-fuselage D-Day Black and White invasion stripes. The fuselage side code has a rounded style 8 which was later changed.

Nose Development

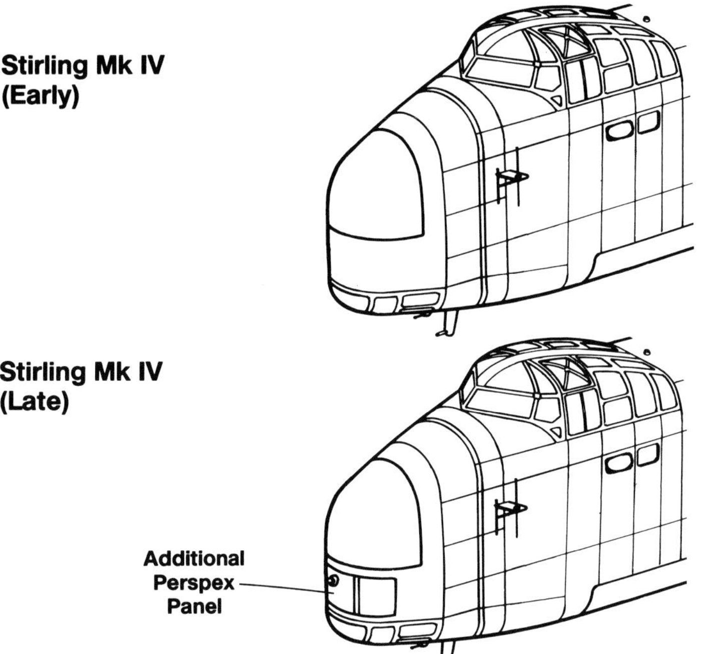

V8-F of No 570 Squadron has been modified with an additional Perspex panel installed in the nose below the nose cap to enhance forward visibility. The D-Day stripes have been over-painted and the 8 in the squadron code has been changed to a square style. *Rebecca* blind landing aid antennas are carried on the fuselage ahead of cockpit.

Glorious Beer, a Stirling Mk IV of No 295 Squadron Mk IV is parked and chocked on its dispersal bay at Rivenhall in East Anglia as its crew stands by for inspection. The aircraft still carries traces of its D-Day invasion stripes underneath the port wing.

Members of No 295 Squadron pose in front of *Glorious Beer*. The nose art reveals the squadron's missions; (top row) daggers, windmills and mountain indicate SOE operations in France, Holland and Norway; (second row) bombs denote bombing raids, while the glider represents Operation VARSITY (Rhine Crossing); (bottom row) daggers with Danish flags are for SOE operations in Denmark.

A trio of Stirling Mk IVs of the Central Navigation School (Summerside) start their engines on a Canadian airfield during June of 1944. The fairing under the rear fuselage houses the H2S radar antenna. The Stirling in the foreground is believed to be LK589 which returned to Britain and served with Nos 295 and 570 Squadrons at Rivenhall.

H2S Radome

Carried On Some Stirling Mk IIIs and Mk IVs

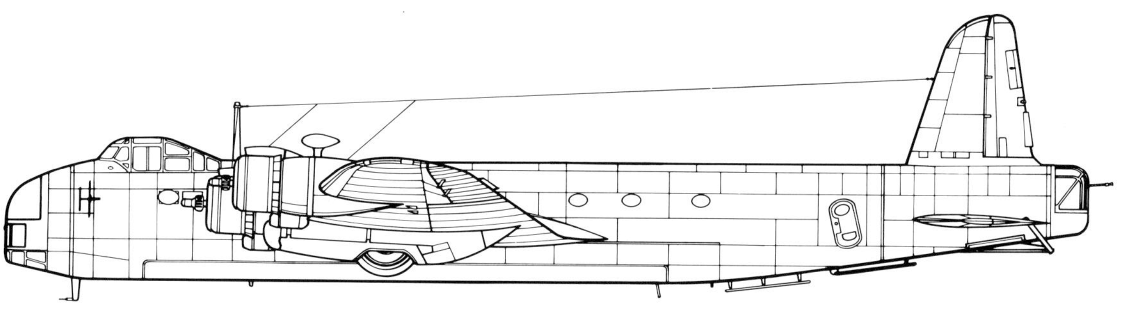

Specifications

Short Stirling Mk IV

Wingspan .... 99 feet 1 inch
Length .... 87 feet 3 inches
Height .... 22 feet 9 inches
Empty Weight .... 43,200 pounds
Maximum Weight .... 77,000 pounds
Powerplant .... Four 1,635 hp Bristol Hercules XIV air cooled radial engines.

Armament .... Four .303 Browning machine guns in tail turret. For bombing missions, 17,000 pounds of bombs could be carried.

Performance

Maximum Speed .... 270 mph
Service ceiling .... 19,000 feet
Range .... 2,360 miles
Crew .... Five

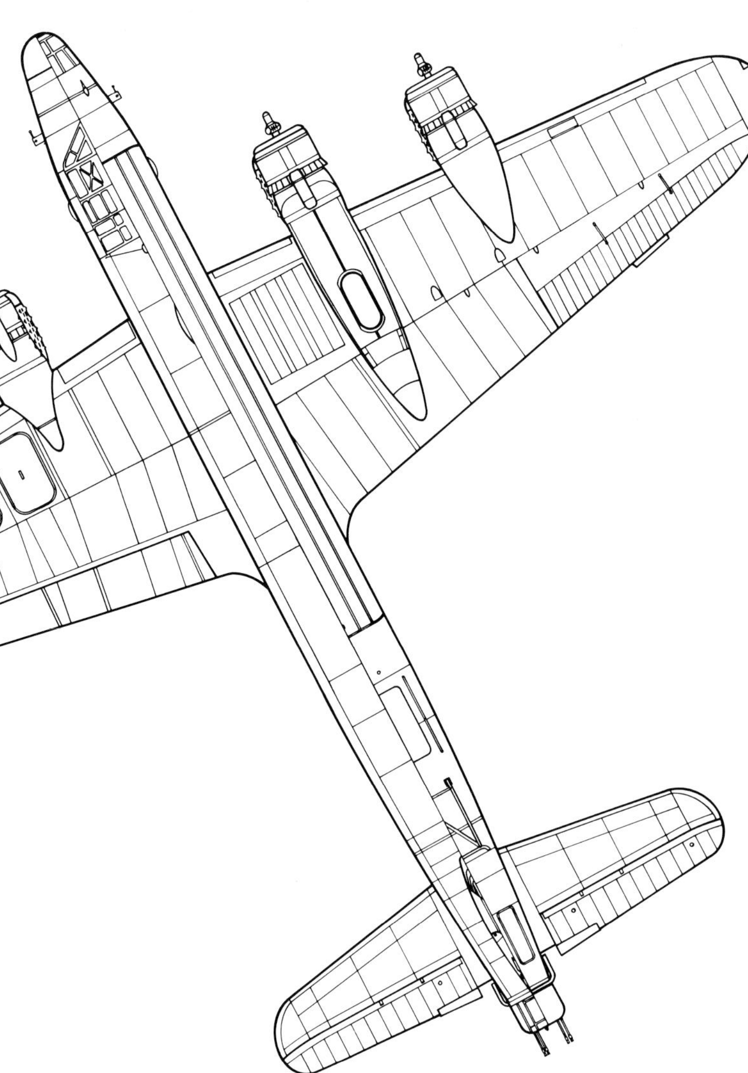

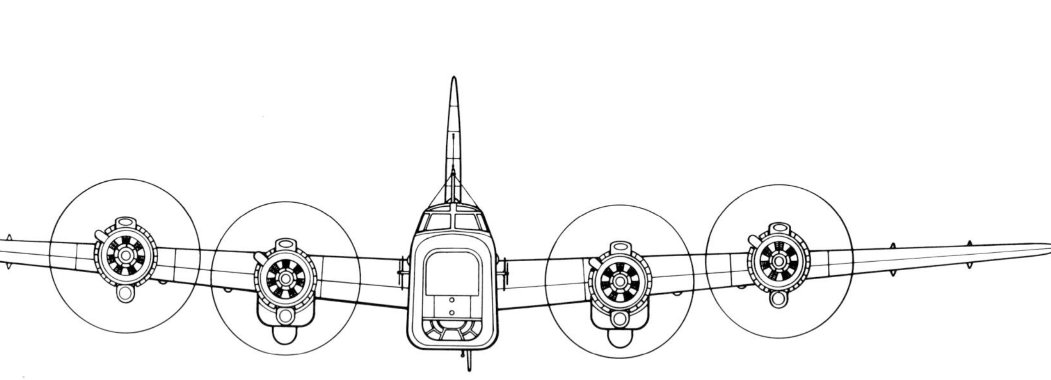

This Stirling Mk IV (EF317) was the first of a production batch produced during December of 1943. These aircraft never saw front line squadron service and were finally SOC between 1945 and 1947. This aircraft is unusual in that it still carries twin pitot tube masts under the nose.

Rolls of Summerfield tracking, used for temporary airfield surfaces, surround this RAF SGT equipped with a signal lamp on an airfield in Europe, as a No 570 Squadron Stirling Mk IV taxies past.

A Stirling Mk IV of No 196 Squadron loads Displaced Persons (refugees) at Prague, Czechoslovakia after the war ended. The aircraft on the ramp in the background are Soviet Air Force Yak fighters.

Commonwealth ex-POWs wait to board Stirling Mk IVs of No 299 Squadron for an airlift back to England. Stirling squadrons played an important role in the airlift of former POWs from all over Europe back to English soil.

This Stirling Mk IV carries an inscription on the fuselage in White identifying it as the 1,000th airframe manufactured by Short's Belfast plant. This aircraft has not had the glider towing yoke installed on the rear fuselage, but has had the strop guard mounted on the fuselage underside in front of the tail wheel.

Because of the possibility of overheating the engines while towing heavy glider loads, a number of Stirling Mk IVs were equipped with cooling fans and propeller spinners. This aircraft is also configured with the late nose section with its additional perspex panels.

Engine Fan

Stirling Mk IV (Early)

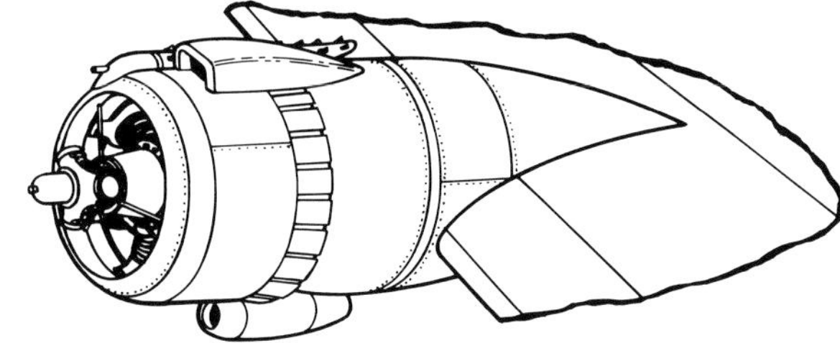

Stirling Mk IV (Late)

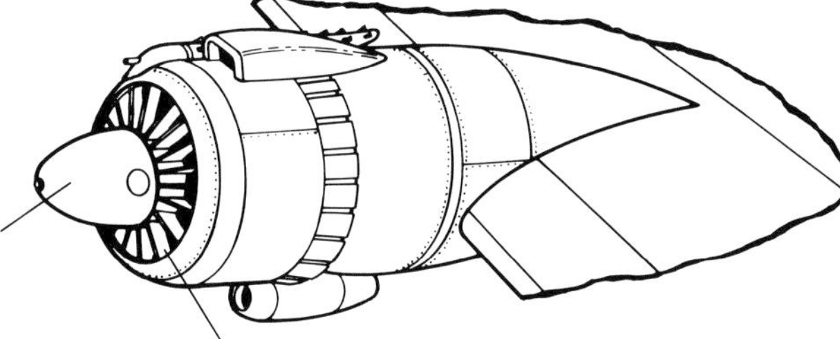

Stirling Mk V

During 1943, Short began planning for a civil freight/passenger variant of the Stirling for the post war civil market. These plans eventually led to the Stirling Mk V, which was a conversion of the Stirling Mk III airframe, optimized for carrying passengers and cargo.

The prototype Mk V (Specification C18/43) was a standard Stirling Mk III airframe (LJ530) with the nose turret and bomb-aimer's position replaced with a sloped, wedge-shaped fairing, capped with a clear perspex dome. The nose section forward of the cockpit was hinged at the top and opened upward to permit loading of over sized cargo. A retractable beam block and tackle frame was located just behind the hinge point and was used to open the nose section. The pitot tube mast was relocated slightly forward from its position on the Mk III.

The top turret and tail turrets were deleted and faired over, with the tail turret having an extended fairing with two vertical ribbed reinforcing frames (although from available information it appears that these ribs were not installed on the prototype or first two production aircraft PJ878/PJ879) and a small perspex window. For loading large cargo, a nine foot six inch by five foot one inch door was installed in the starboard side of the fuselage, just to the rear of the bomb bay. This door was hinged at the bottom and opened downward and outward forming a loading ramp. The fuselage windows were changed, being increased to eight on the port side and seven on the starboard side, with a close grouping of four and five respectively above the wing roots where the passenger section was located.

The Mk V was ordered into production and a contract was placed for 160 aircraft, with the first two production aircraft being delivered to No 23 Maintenance Unit (MU) based at Aldergrove during September of 1944. Both aircraft were camouflaged; however, they carried a scheme that contrasted with the drab Bomber Command scheme carried by their predecessors. The new camouflage consisted of Dark Green and Medium Grey uppersurfaces over Azure Blue lowersurfaces. The requirement for camouflage schemes remained in effect until VE-Day. Shortly after the war ended, one Mk V (PJ944) was experimentally stripped of its paint and the reduction in weight and drag increased the aircraft's cruising speed to 190 mph. Eventually, most Stirling Mk Vs were stripped and flew in a bare metal finish.

The Stirling Mk V was powered by the 1,635 hp Hercules XVI air cooled radial engines and had a maximum speed 280 mph, a range of 3,000 miles and a service ceiling of 18,000 feet. Empty weight was 43,500 pounds and maximum weight was 70,000 pounds. It could carry mixed cargo/passenger loads, with a maximum passenger seating for up to forty passengers, although on normal operations fourteen seats were usually fitted in the passenger compartment. Alternatively, twenty paratroops and their equipment could be carried and for the medical evacuation role, twelve stretchers could be fitted along with fourteen seated patients. The crew consisted of five men, two pilots, navigator, flight engineer and load master.

With the civil market in mind, during May of 1945, one Mk V (PJ958) was soundproofed and equipped to carry thirty passengers in the hopes of winning a contract from British Overseas Airways Corporation (BOAC). At this same time, however, Handley Page had completed conversion of the Halifax to a freight/passenger aircraft, with the freight carried in a detachable pannier slung under the bomb bay area. Unfortunately for Shorts, the Halifax conversion was selected by BOAC to meet its long range transport requirements.

It was to be another two years before the Mk V entered civil service when twelve aircraft were purchased by a Belgian company, Trans-Air. The ex-military aircraft were refurbished by the Airtech company during 1947 and delivered in groups of six. They were used on charter flights to China and the Far East; however, their careers were short and all were withdrawn from service within a year.

The RAF used the majority of the Stirling Mk Vs produced and its operational career was to span a year and a half in the period between late 1944 and mid-1946. The first squadron to operate the Stirling Mk V was No 46 Squadron, which was followed almost immediately by No 242 Squadron. These two squadrons were followed by No 51 Squadron in June of 1945. The last Mk V squadron was No 158 Squadron, although two Heavy Freight Flights, Nos 1588 and 1589 operated in opposite directions between Britain and India, from bases in the Middle East.

The Stirling Mk V was used primarily to establish regular service between the UK, India and the Far East. Trips between India and the UK would normally take some twelve days, with freight loads running approximately 5,290 pounds and passenger loads usually consisting of seventeen passengers. Flights were conducted on alternate days until October of 1945 when they were reduced to three per week.

The Mk V was briefly used by No 196 Squadron during early 1946; however, by this time, the aircraft was rapidly being phased out of service with only No 46 Squadron, flying the India route, and the two HFF units remaining. No 1588 HFF was the last active Stirling Mk V unit, finally retiring the aircraft during July of 1946. During its eighteen months of service, the MK V had carried out a sizeable number of freight and troop movements, but the obvious superiority of the Avro York finally overtook what was, after all, a limited capability conversion of a basic bomber design.

The Stirling Mk V prototype featured a lengthened and streamlined nose section ending in a clear perspex nose cap. The prototype also carried a new camouflage scheme of Dark Green and Grey uppersurfaces over Azure Blue undersurfaces.

A Stirling Mk V (PK124) of No 51 Squadron is pushed down the runway of an Indian airfield. The Stirling Mk V had the tail turret area faired over and the engine nacelles were modified with the exhaust stacks being located further down on the cowling sides.

A camouflaged Stirling Mk V of an unidentified squadron sets on the ramp at Lahore, India, during 1946. Stirlings were used to fly the India route, with the trip usually taking some twelve days to complete. (Ken Turner)

Nose Development

Stirling Mk III

Stirling Mk V

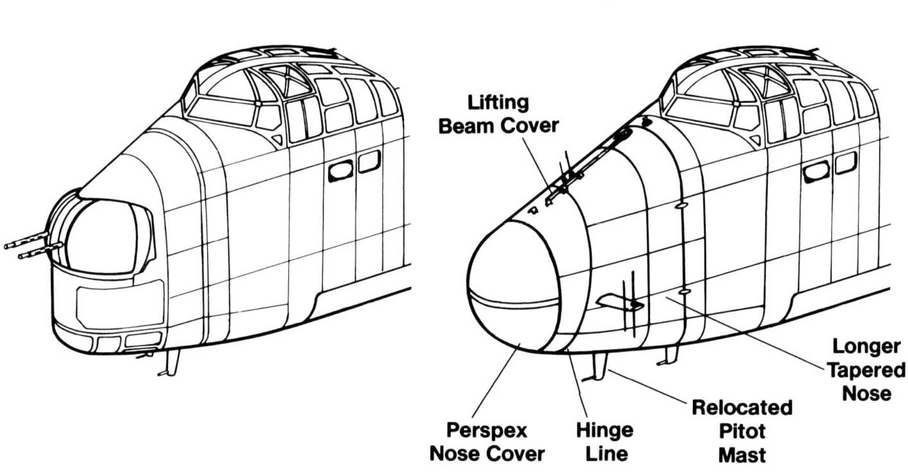

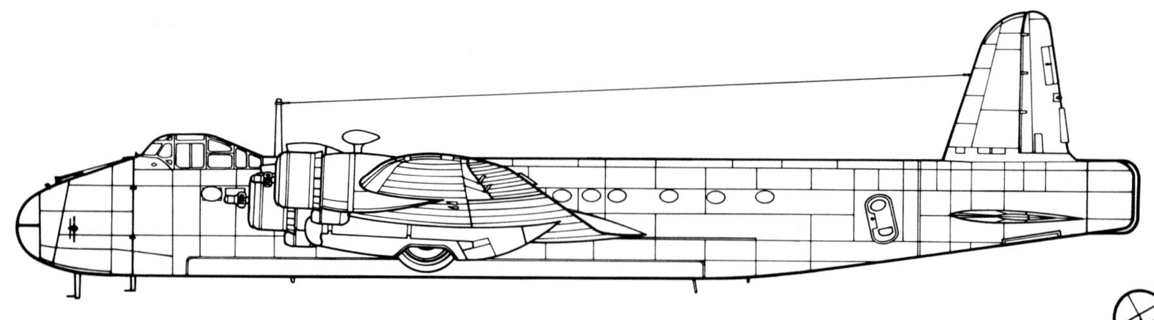

Specifications

Short Stirling Mk V

Wingspan .... 99 feet 1 inch
Length .... 90 feet 6 ¾ inches
Height .... 22 feet 9 inches
Empty Weight .... 43,500 pounds
Maximum Weight .... 70,000 pounds
Powerplants .... Four 1,635 hp Bristol Hercules XVI air cooled radial engines.

Armament .... None

Performance

Maximum Speed .... 280 mph
Service ceiling .... 18,000 feet
Range .... 3,000 miles
Crew .... Five

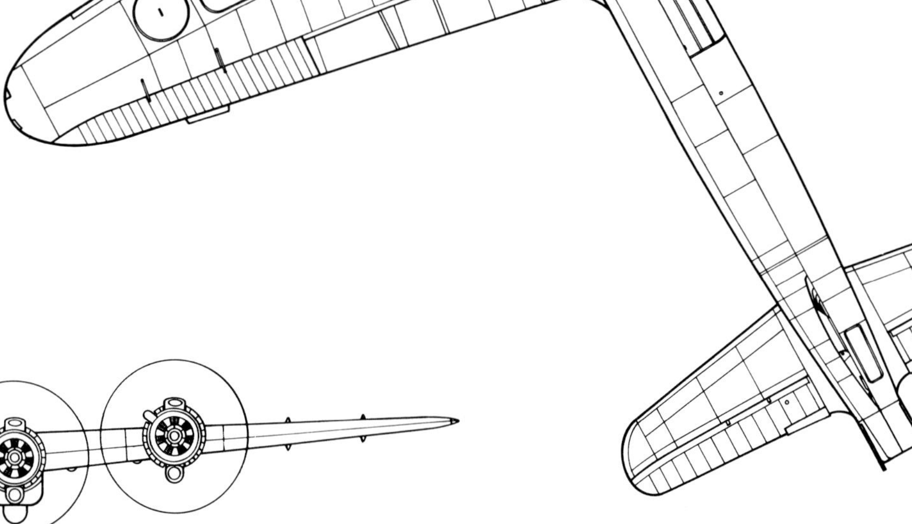

(Above) No 242 Squadron at Stoney Cross was the second Stirling unit convert to the Mk V and this aircraft shows this squadron's method of displaying the squadron and aircraft code letters. The code is carried as small Black letters on each side of the nose. Even though the Mk V was strictly a transport, it retained the bomb bay doors and controls.

(Below) This Stirling Mk V (PJ988) served with both Nos 242 and 46 Squadrons. The Stirling is parked on a French air field (probably Toulouse) during the Summer of 1945 while in transit from Britain to North Africa. The outlined area on the rear fuselage is the cargo door. The Halifax in background is carrying a cargo pannier under the fuselage.

(Above) This bare metal Stirling Mk V of No 196 squadron on final approach to an unidentified airfield during January of 1946 has a bullet ADF antenna and large astrodome on the upper fuselage spine. Late production Mk Vs were delivered in either a White or Natural Metal finish.

(Below) This Stirling Mk V of No 46 Squadron (PK173) crashed on takeoff from St. Thomas Mount, India on 13 November 1945. The collapse of the undercarriage has caused the propellers to be bent over and the flaps to be dented and holed.

Tail Fairing

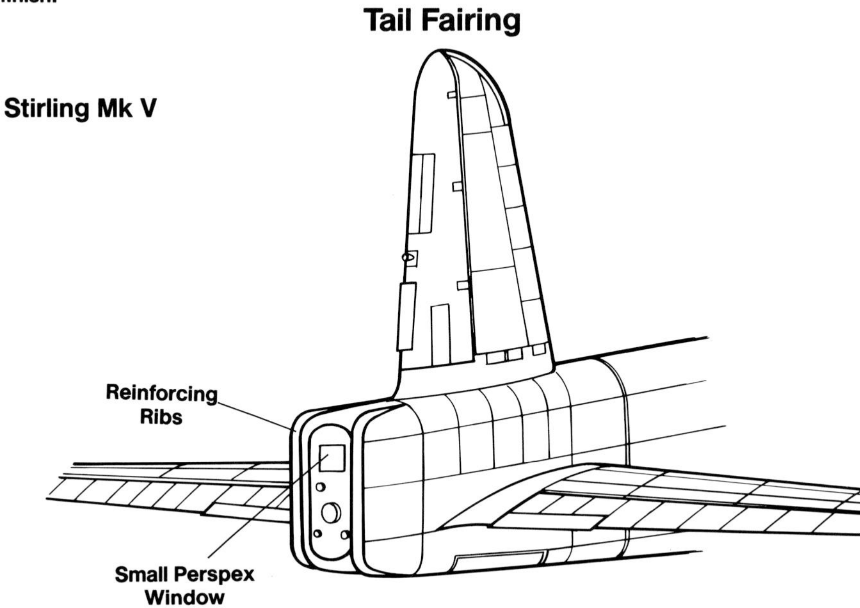

The downward opening cargo door in the fuselage side of the Stirling Mk V was equipped with loading ramps and was braced by twin metal support rods when in use. The twin tailwheels are equipped with special tires designed to prevent swinging on takeoff or landing. The larger tires required the tail wheel well doors to be bulged.

Window Arrangement

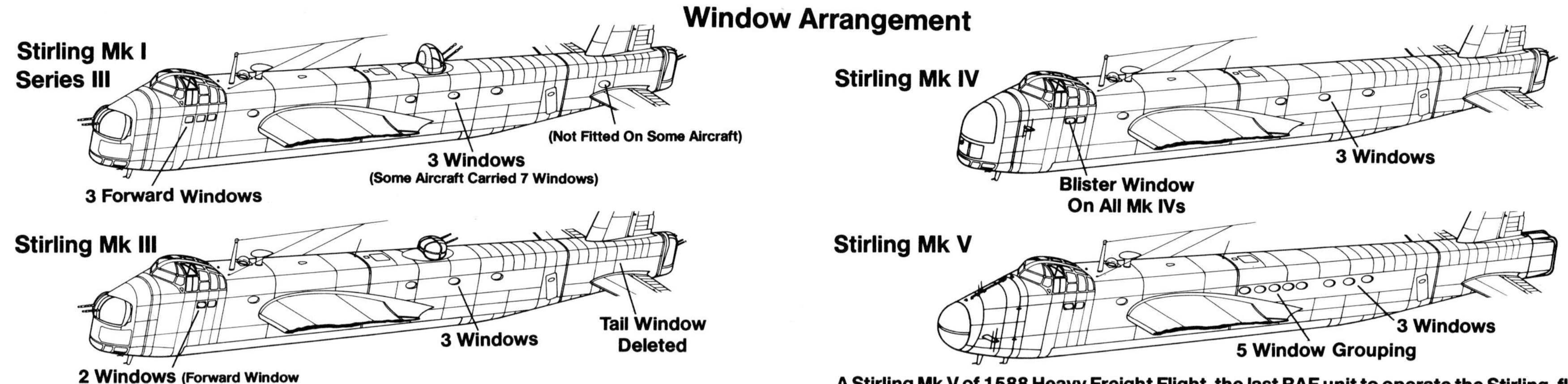

A Stirling Mk V of 1588 Heavy Freight Flight, the last RAF unit to operate the Stirling, flies low over the water off Juhu beach near Santa Cruz, India during April of 1946. Three months later the unit retired the last of its Stirlings from active service.

One of the twelve Mk Vs (OO-XAD) refurbished by Airtech and operated by the Belgium Trans-Air company rests on the ground at Tours, France. The civil registration and company name was painted on the aircraft in Black.

Exhaust Stacks

Stirling Mk III

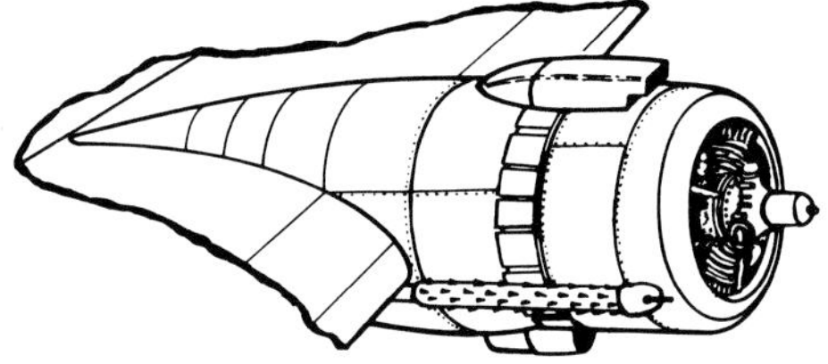

Stirling Mk V
(Outboard Engines Only)

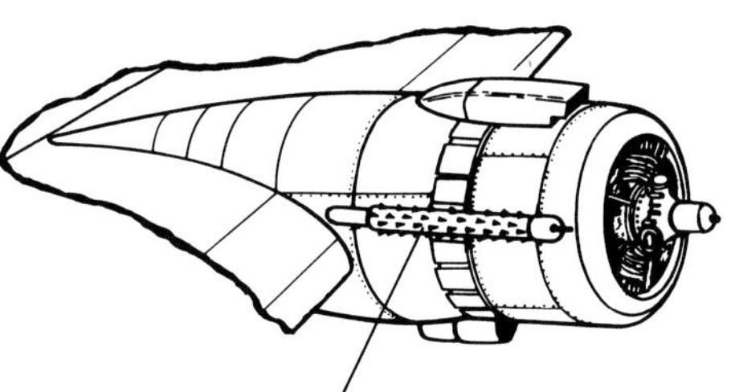

OO-XAV was an ex-RAF aircraft (PK174) which saw service with Trans-Air before being sold to a second Belgium company, Air Transport S.A. It is believed that this is one of the three Stirling Mk Vs later sold to the Egyptian Air Force during 1948. Reportedly, these were converted back into bombers for use against Israel.

RAF Aircraft

From Squadron/Signal

1039 

1072 

1076 

1088 

squadron/signal publications